YOUR BEST FOOT FORWARD

YOUR BEST

Social Usage for

FOOT
FORWARD

Young Moderns

DOROTHY C. STRATTON
Executive Director,
Girl Scouts of the United States of America

HELEN B. SCHLEMAN
Dean of Women, Purdue University

McGRAW-HILL BOOK COMPANY, INC.
New York   Toronto   London

Dedicated to the students in coeducational colleges from Maine to California who sent us the questions and helped us with the answers.

PREFACE

THIS BOOK tries to answer those questions of social usage which many members of the younger generation meet frequently during their daily life. It is addressed to those young people who have a major interest in dating, care about improving their table manners, entertain and visit friends, meet a great many new people, and would like to do all these things easily. It is not a manual for the coming-out parties of debutantes nor does it contain information as to the best methods of managing a household of fifteen servants. These matters are adequately covered elsewhere. It deals with the everyday problems of young Americans in school and out of school.

Which problems of social usage are worth consideration? This question must be answered by anyone who proposes to treat the subject of social usage in a practical manner. For the purposes of this book, we have judged those questions in social usage to be important which young people themselves say they would like to have answered. We have attempted to ascertain these questions by obtaining from a sampling of the younger generation those questions of social usage which were causing them difficulty. This present volume is based upon (1) the questions submitted in 1939 by the original sampling of the student population in nine coeducational colleges and universities throughout the country, (2) the questions submitted in 1950 by a second sampling of the student population in twelve coeducational colleges and universities, and (3) the questions submitted by samplings of the participants in the annual 4-H Leadership Training Schools of Indiana from 1949 through 1954. College students make up the larger part of the total of all samplings because we believed that questions asked by them would be representative not only of problems peculiar to college campuses but also of those which students meet as part of the general population and, therefore, to some extent at least, of young people in general. This assumption was confirmed by the fact that there was no particular difference between the sorts of questions submitted by the samplings of young people made up entirely of college students and those submitted by the 4-H Leadership Training School participants, which included both boys and girls attending colleges and those not in attendance.

The young people were asked to jot down those questions in social usage which had puzzled them. It was suggested that the questions might include any areas of social behavior, such as dating, dances, table manners, receptions, manners on the street, in public places, and so on. No specific questions were suggested and certain areas, e.g., introductions, were not included in the list. Over 6,200 questions were submitted by the original sampling of students, some 3,200 by the second sampling of students, and approximately 1,000 by the sampling of the 4-H Leadership School participants. In all, well over 10,000 questions covering every phase of the social relationship of young people have been considered.

A tabulation of these questions showed clearly the areas of social usage that most frequently cause difficulty. Not only were these areas high in the aggregate but they were high for each institution represented. For example, questions on introductions rank first in frequency in two colleges and second in five in the first survey. This area was also high in frequency in the subsequent questions collected. In fact, there was no marked difference in the types of questions nor the areas of social usage included in the questions asked by young people in 1950 to 1954 from those asked earlier, except in one particular. Members of the current generation of young people have introduced questions, in fact many questions, in an area scarcely mentioned previously—that of engagements and weddings of college students. This is an understandable reflection of a social era that is seeing the lowest average marriage age in the history of the country. The large areas in which questions were asked most frequently form the chapter headings of this book.

The questions are of three general kinds:

1. Those in areas in which social practice is well defined and generally accepted.

2. Those in areas of everyday social contacts not usually covered in standard books of etiquette.

3. Those concerned with areas of social relationships between young men and young women in which practices are changing relatively rapidly.

Questions in the first two areas, those in which social practice is well defined and everyday sorts of problems, were relatively easy to answer by reliance upon observable practice, by reference to authorities, by day-to-day discussion with students, and by using what we like to think of as the dictates of common sense.

Questions in the third area, in which practices are in process of relatively rapid change, were considerably more difficult. It was obvious from the wording of the questions that students wanted to know the practices acceptable to their contemporaries, not those handed down by an authority. In order to have some valid basis for answering these questions we sampled—at two different times— through the aid of Mortar Board, national honorary organization for senior women, the opinion of college leaders, both men and women, on coeducational college campuses. The first sampling was made from fifty-nine campuses. The second was made from seventy-one campuses. The present volume reflects the opinion of these college leaders as to what constitutes current accepted practice as expressed in the more recent survey and in subsequent discussions with students in social-usage discussion panels and conferences. We consider these answers significant not only because we believe that student leaders know what is accepted practice on their own campuses but because we believe that their opinions carry the weight of authority with their contemporaries.

We present this material as our interpretation of the current social code as it applies to everyday problems. We hope that anyone of the younger generation reading it will learn as much as we have learned in its preparation.

DOROTHY C. STRATTON *and* HELEN B. SCHLEMAN

ACKNOWLEDGMENTS

Our greatest debt is to the students, both men and women, in the following colleges and universities who sent us the questions on which this book is based: Alfred University; State University Teachers College, Cortland, N.Y.; DePauw University; Fort Hays Kansas State College; Municipal University of Wichita; State University College for Teachers, Albany, N.Y.; State Teachers College, Mansfield, Pennsylvania; Pennsylvania State University; Purdue University; Santa Barbara College of the University of California; University of Iowa; University of Kentucky; University of Louisville; University of Maine; University of Maryland; University of Minnesota; University of Nebraska; University of Wisconsin; and Wayne University.

We are indebted to the members of Mortar Board, national honorary organization for senior women, as well as to the men leaders on more than seventy college campuses who gave us the viewpoints of their contemporaries and interpreted for us current practice in areas of social usage that are rapidly changing.

To the hundreds of Purdue students with whom we discussed student questions and to those who read and criticized portions of the manuscript we express our sincere appreciation.

We are especially indebted to the 1954 president of the Purdue Chapter of Mortar Board, Judy Kirkpatrick McKinney, and to the 1954 president of the Purdue Associated Women Students, Jane McEllhiney Stein, for their contributions to the chapter on engagements and weddings based on their own experience.

We acknowledge the valuable assistance of Pat di Sernia, fashion editor of *The American Girl*, in the chapter on personal appearance; of Betty Thomas, coordinator of placement for women, Purdue University, in the section on dress and grooming for a business interview; and of Betty Bauer Lambert, travel representative, Racquet & Tennis Club, New York, in the chapter on travel.

We are greatly indebted to Helen Sprowls for intelligent assistance in the preparation of the manuscript.

CONTENTS

YOUR BEST FOOT FORWARD

Chapter One

YOU AND SOCIAL
USAGE

S OCIAL USAGE is one section of that large area of social customs
and traditions by which society seeks to socialize the individual and to regulate social intercourse. Social customs are to
society what habits are to the individual. They are the ways in
which society in general performs certain acts; and, like habits
in the individual, are changed only by considerable effort. They
exist for the purpose of reducing friction and of making social
relationships pleasant.

Social usage is not something reserved for families with five
servants or for individuals whose names appear in the society
columns. Each person employs social usage, as he uses his native
language, every day of his life. It is a part of our contemporary
culture and as such is important to every individual regardless
of his education, social status, or financial condition.

Our social usages are not necessarily the best of all possible
social usages in the best of all possible worlds. It might well
be that, if our society were to start anew tomorrow and all traditions and customs were to be forgotten, new and better social
usages might be evolved, just as better cities might be con-
structed if architects and city planners did not have to build
around the old mistakes. At any given time, current social usage
carries with it some outmoded practices and is also introducing new practices in new areas. Sooner or later, sectors of social
usage in which practice is outmoded feel the stress of changed
conditions, and accepted usage is modified to meet the new
situations. In our present-day society, social usage is a dynamic,
changing social front.

SOCIAL USAGES DO CHANGE

For proof of the rapidity with which our social customs change, we have only to amuse ourselves by reading an etiquette book of ninety years ago. One that gives an illuminating picture of life as it was lived in the United States at the time of the Civil War is *The Ladies' Guide to True Politeness and Correct Manners,* by "Miss Leslie." In 1864, no lady walked alone after dark, called a gentleman by his first name, carried on a correspondence with any male except her husband or a relative, laid a bet, mentioned the word "stomach" in polite society, or permitted her caller to remain later than ten o'clock. Gentlemen then as now were presented to ladies in introductions but in a much more formal manner. The form was, "Miss Smith, permit me to make you acquainted with Mr. Jones." A lady is admonished by Miss Leslie that there is nothing amusing in another person's falling on the ice and that it is more feminine on witnessing such a sight to utter an involuntary scream than a shout of laughter. In an omnibus, a lady requests a gentleman to give her fare to the driver. When having dinner in a hotel, she may dispense with her black mittens; she must not cut her pie with her fork alone, but she must use both knife and fork.

It would be interesting, indeed, if we could trace the causes of the changes in these social usages; but we know little about them. We do know that scientific inventions which affect our daily lives are one important factor in changing our customs. New situations demand new solutions and modify old ones. The automobile, the radio, the airplane, the telephone and television have affected our dress and our speech. Changing economic conditions have altered the status of women. Apartment houses with their limitations on living space, the trend to informal living, and the cost of domestic labor have profoundly modified the type of hospitality that most families can offer.

We know, too, that customs are not changed by edict but by a gradual breaking away from those usages which no longer appear to be useful under changed conditions. Myerson, in his *Social Psychology*, points out that customs change when they become so extreme as to be a handicap in the struggle for existence and cites as examples of current usages that are in this classification, but have not yet been changed, the high-heeled shoes still worn by women and the heavy coat and collar and tie worn by men even in hot weather.

With the present rate of scientific invention, it seems probable that the rate of change in social customs will continue to be accelerated. These changes are desirable and indicate that we live in a dynamic, not a static, society. If, ninety years from now, some young person were to brush the dust and cobwebs from this book and read of the customs of today, there is little doubt that they would appear more amusing and more outmoded to him than those of 1864 seem to us. So, of course, would our houses, our fashions, our automobiles, our subways, and our refrigerators seem, could this same young person of the twenty-first century see them. For us, however, they are integral parts of our daily life and are, therefore, important.

YOU AND SOCIAL USAGE

You may view social regulations as fetters which are irksome to bear and which hamper your individual freedom at every turn. If you take this point of view, you will expend valuable time and energy "kicking against the pricks" and in all probability will not modify the social mores to an appreciable extent. John Dewey pointed out that the part played by custom in shaping the behavior of the individual, as over against any way in which he can affect traditional custom, is as the proportion of the total vocabulary of his mother tongue over against those words of his own baby talk that are taken into the vernacular of his family.

On the other hand, you may regard social customs as essential to the smooth conduct of social intercourse and be willing to accept gracefully the restrictions imposed upon you. If you take this position, you will learn the rules of the game as you do those of an athletic contest or as you have your three R's. Once they are automatic, you can be free from concern about them and can devote your attention to the more interesting aspects of social contacts.

The story is told of Margaret Fuller that she once said she had decided to accept the universe. Carlyle, upon hearing of this, remarked, "She had better." Sooner or later, each of us has to come to this conclusion about social usage as well as about more important aspects of life. Having decided to accept social customs in general as we find them, we are free to turn our attention to the essence of contact between persons—good human relationships. In the same way, a typist, after she has facility on the keyboard, turns her attention to the material, not the mechanics.

A thorough knowledge of current social usage gives you a feeling of personal security which one who is constantly worried about his next move cannot have. As the knowledge that she is suitably dressed for the occasion gives to a woman a feeling of self-assurance in a difficult social situation, so the certainty of knowing what is expected of you in specific situations helps to ease tension and to relieve you of embarrassment and of worry.

No thinking person would maintain that the most important characteristic of a man or a woman is the ability to make an introduction smoothly or that a man is worthy of one's friendship because he can eat lobster gracefully. Among the most important qualities about an individual are, of course, his integrity, his sense of fair play, his regard for the rights of others, his willingness to cooperate with others, his sense of values. It should be remembered, however, that the so-called rules of social usage are built upon these foundations. Respect for the rights of others is the cornerstone upon which social intercourse is built. A truly well-bred person never hesitates to break any rule of etiquette rather than hurt another person's feelings.

SOCIAL USAGE A MEANS, NOT AN END

Techniques of social usage should always be regarded as a means, not as an end. The end to be achieved is happy, satisfactory social relationships. The techniques of social usage assist one to achieve this goal. They are not substitutes for more basic personal qualities. Unfortunately, you cannot tell by looking at another person whether he is honest or considerate or cooperative, nor can he accurately estimate these qualities in you. Such characteristics are observable only through close acquaintanceship. A person's knowledge of social usage or his lack of it is readily apparent in a casual meeting and may condition your attitude toward him, and in like manner your actions affect him favorably or unfavorably. Surface evidences of cultivation are not to be lightly regarded.

It is important to learn social usages in order that you may be welcome at home, in other people's homes, and in general society. All of us wish our social behavior to be such that other people will be attracted to us rather than repelled. All of us like to be liked. We do not wish to offend others consciously or unconsciously. It is as natural for us to want to please others as it is for us to want food. Moreover, psychologists tell us that satisfying social relationships are vital to the development of an adequate personality. We now know that the knowledge of how to act in social situations is one of the determining factors in the reaction of other people toward us. For example, Thomas found that the five traits mentioned most frequently by women in explaining their liking for men were intelligence, consideration, kindliness, cheerfulness, and mannerliness. Good social usage requires the expression of all these traits.

HOW TO DEVELOP SOCIAL SKILLS

We used to believe that we learned skills purely by repetition. Take, for example, the problem of learning to play tennis. We thought that if one wanted to learn to be a good tennis player, he simply practiced for hours every day. The fact is now rather well established that repetition or practice alone will not necessarily bring marked improvement in tennis or in other skills. At least three other factors must be present. The first is a genuine desire to improve. The second is a knowledge of the correct way of doing the particular skill to be learned. The third is a critical attitude toward the practice period, which makes one strive constantly to eliminate errors. The learning period may be shortened considerably if these three factors are present.

The fact that you are reading this book indicates a desire on your part to improve your social skills—the first essential of learning. You will find in this book suggestions as to the correct way of doing the particular social skills that you wish to learn. You can rehearse these at home or with your friends, then try out your skills in social situations, evaluate your efforts, and try for a smoother performance at a later date. No individual is born with social skills. He learns them throughout his entire lifetime. The person who learns them most readily is usually he who wants to learn, who studies through books and through observation how to improve his skills, and who critically evaluates his performance. Social skills can be learned!

Chapter Two

INTRODUCTIONS

WHAT DO YOU DO *if you can't remember the name of one of the persons whom you are introducing? about rising when you are introduced to an older person? when you are introduced to someone whom you have just met? if you are wearing gloves when you are introduced? Do you shake hands, say "Excuse my glove," not mention it, or just not shake hands? if other couples join your group and no one introduces you?*

HOW SHOULD YOU *acknowledge an introduction? introduce your parents to the President of the University? introduce a newcomer to a roomful of people? introduce your date to two other couples when she doesn't know any of the others? introduce a clergyman? introduce another girl and your sister to each other?*

DOES *a man always shake hands with another man? What does he do when he is introduced to a woman? a woman shake hands with another woman? a woman rise when she meets another woman her own age? An older man? being in class with a person serve as an introduction? one use academic titles—Professor, Doctor, Dean—in making introductions?*

EVERYONE who does not lead the life of a hermit finds that making and acknowledging introductions is an inescapable part of his everyday life. The suggestions that follow are designed to put you at your ease when you find yourself called upon to introduce your mother, your father, your date for the evening, your house guest, or anyone else for that matter.

The custom of making introductions is a device for placing social intercourse upon a friendly basis. Simply reading about how to do it will not, however, necessarily make you at ease in a social situation that requires you to demonstrate your knowledge. You should practice on your friends, or on the furniture if necessary, until the accepted forms for introductions come automatically when needed. Create opportunities to try out your skill, remembering that ease comes only with practice.

There are, in general, three kinds of introductions: introductions between men and women, introductions between members of the same sex, and introductions of an individual to a group. One rule which is without exception in individual introductions is: *Mention first the name of the person to whom deference is being shown.*

The principle underlying all introductions between men and women is that it is an honor for a man to be introduced to a woman; therefore, *the woman's name is mentioned first.* The usual form would be:

You: "Mrs. Brown, may I introduce Mr. Loring?"
Mrs. Brown: "How do you do, Mr. Loring?"
Mr. Loring: "How do you do, Mrs. Brown?"

An informal introduction suitable for school or home situations would be:

You: "Mary, this is John Sackett, who is a sophomore at Michigan." (*Turning to John*) "This is Mary Burns, John."
Mary: "How do you do, Mr. Sackett?"
John: "How do you do, Miss Burns?"

If you and Mary were with a group of your contemporaries all of whom were on a first name basis with each other, Mary would no doubt size up the situation and say, "Hello, John," and John would then reply, "Hello, Mary." Groups of college students frequently accept a newcomer into their group in this informal fashion with no time lost, but don't take any chances on using this form in a business situation or in one that is the least bit formal.

If you were introducing a very distinguished man or an elderly man to a young woman and felt that you wished to honor the man, you might choose to say: "Mr. Distinguished [or Mr. Seventy-five], may I introduce Miss Monroe?" [or Emily Monroe, if the entire name would identify her more clearly]. This form of introduction would be the rare exception, however, and would more likely be used by a woman introducing another woman than by a man making the introduction.

Age, rank, and degree of distinction are the determining factors in introductions between members of the same sex. Deference is shown the older person, the person of higher rank, the person of distinction. *A young woman is introduced to an older woman; mention the older woman's name first. A young man is introduced to an older man; mention the older man's name first. A person of moderate attainments is introduced to a distinguished personage; mention the distinguished person's name first.* If two persons of the same sex, age group, rank, and degree of distinction are being introduced, the order of introductions is a matter of choice. A great many introductions are of this kind.

A young woman is introduced to an older woman:

You: "Mrs. Dowager, this is Miss Twenty" or "This is Sally Twenty."
Mrs. Dowager: "How do you do, Miss Twenty?" or "How do you do, Sally?"
Sally: "How do you do, Mrs. Dowager?"

A young man is introduced to an older man:

You: "Mr. Sixty-five, may I introduce Mr. Twenty?" or "May I introduce Robert Twenty?"
Mr. Sixty-five (extending his hand): "How do you do, Mr. Twenty?" or "How do you do, Robert?"

Robert (accepting the proffered hand): "How do you do, sir?" or "How do you do, Mr. Sixty-five?"

A person of lesser rank is introduced to one of higher rank:

You: "Major Burton, may I introduce Lieutenant Sayres?"
Major Burton (shaking hands): "How do you do, Lieutenant Sayres?"
Lieutenant Sayres: "How do you do, Major Burton?" or "How do you do, sir?"

This custom is observed more rigidly in military circles and in official life than elsewhere.

A person of ordinary attainments is introduced to a person of distinction:

You: "Mr. Personage, may I introduce Mr. Jones?"
Mr. Personage (shaking hands): "How do you do, Mr. Jones?"
Mr. Jones: "How do you do, Mr. Personage?"

A person is introduced to a group in the order in which they are sitting or standing, and for the sake of brevity and simplicity his name is mentioned first:

You to a Group: "I should like to introduce Mr. Brown: Miss Burgess, Mr. Shearer, Miss Grey, Mrs. Cole."

It is perfectly good form to introduce the women first and then the men, but it is sometimes a more clumsy procedure. Mr. Brown acknowledges each introduction with "How do you do?" and each member of the group does likewise. It is awkward to introduce one person to an entire roomful of people. It is better to introduce him to a few at a time.

When introducing a man and a woman, mention the woman's name first; a younger person and an older person, mention the older person's name first; a person of great distinction and one of less distinction, mention the person of great distinction first; an individual and a group, mention the individual's name first and then go around the group in order just as they happen to be seated or standing.

FORMS OF INTRODUCTION

All the following forms of introduction are equally correct: "May I present?" "May I introduce?" "I should like to introduce"; "This is"; "Mr. Jones, Mr. Smith"; "Do you know?" "Have you met?" The first three are the most formal, the second two less formal, and the last two least formal of all. Into the discard are "Shake hands with," "Meet my friend," "I want to make you acquainted with."

It is helpful when you are introducing two people to give them a conversational lead by identifying them for each other if you can do it easily. "Miss Brown, this is Sam Martin [Mr. Martin], who was a member of the Glee Club at Ohio State with your brother Charles."

FORMS OF ACKNOWLEDGMENT

There is practically no opportunity for originality in the acknowledgment of an introduction. One acknowledges any and all introductions with "How-do-you-do?" with or without such additions as "Mrs. Brown," "Dr. Amos," "Professor Carl." If you are really extraordinarily gratified to be introduced to someone, you might add, "I'm very glad to have the opportunity to meet you" or "It is a pleasure to meet you." If you say, "I'm charmed"; "Delighted, I'm sure"; or "Pleased to meet you," your social stock will drop to a new low. The only exception to "How do you do?" might be in an informal situation with your contemporaries in which a "Hello, John" might suffice. As illustrated in the examples given, the person whose name is mentioned first makes the first acknowledgment by speaking first.

WHEN TO RISE FOR AN INTRODUCTION

*"Under what circumstances does a young man remain seated
during an introduction?"*

*"Does a young woman rise when being introduced to another
of the same age? To a woman about ten years older?"*

*"Should a young woman rise when she is being introduced to
a young man?"*

*"When a well-known man is presented to a woman, does she
rise?"*

Nothing short of physical disability excuses a young man
from rising for an introduction to a woman, to an older man,
to a man his own age, or to a younger man. A man always rises
for an introduction.

Some business and professional men and women have fallen
into the habit of remaining seated at their desks when their
receptionist brings a business caller, either man or woman, into
their inner office. This lack of the hospitable gesture of rising
immediately makes the visitor feel like an intruder. If this happens to you, try not to let it disturb your self-confidence. In all
probability the executive has many callers and he feels he
doesn't have time to get up so often. If you remember how you
feel about his carelessness, however, it may keep you from
offending someone when you are sitting on the host's side of
the desk. If you would make the caller feel welcome, whether
you are a man or a woman back of the desk, you will rise in
greeting or for the introduction if one is in order.

The whole matter of women's rising or not rising for introductions has changed considerably over the past decade. Perhaps
the fact that some twenty million women are now working
outside their homes has had some impact upon social usage in
this area as it has in such matters as men's giving up or not giving up bus or subway seats to women. In business and profes-

sional situations women find themselves rising and shaking hands for introductions as a matter of course. This in turn makes such responses natural often in a purely social situation. In any case, there is a lot more rising and shaking hands on the part of women during introductions than there was formerly, and a young woman would do well to be alert to that fact. She certainly rises when an introduction is made to or by an older person, man or woman. She rises whenever she is in any sense in a hostess position, even though she is not the direct hostess herself, as, for instance, when she is in her residence-unit living room and any visitor is being introduced to her. As hostess, she always rises to greet all her guests.

About the only time a young woman would not rise for an introduction would be in a group situation when a contemporary was being introduced and it might be more confusing for her to scramble to her feet than to remain seated.

WHEN TO SHAKE HANDS

"Is handshaking ever necessary?"

"Should a girl offer to shake hands with a boy?"

"Does a man shake hands when being introduced to a group of men?"

"Do women shake hands when being introduced to one another?"

Handshaking is necessary under the following conditions:

1. Whenever anyone extends his hand to you. The gesture is decidedly one of friendliness and cordiality and should be so recognized. No well-bred person ever refuses a proffered hand.
2. When men are introduced to one another. Even when being introduced to a group of men, a man shakes hands with every man in the group, unless circumstances make it very awkward for him to do so.

3. When a host or hostess is greeting the guests, both men and women, or saying good-by.

Women may shake hands when being introduced if they choose to do so. They should anticipate the possibility and should not be taken by surprise if the other person extends his or her hand.

While the initiative for extending the hand when a man and a woman are introduced rests theoretically with the woman, she should be alert to the possibility that the man may extend his hand in a habitual response. If he does, she certainly shakes hands. In any case she may choose to do so if she wishes to.

It is just as important to know how to shake hands as to know when to shake hands. You should strive for a nice balance between a viselike grip which leaves the victim wincing and a limp, unresponsive one which makes the other person feel as if he had touched a damp rubber glove. A handshake is a friendly gesture and should convey to the other person the fact that you are really glad to see him. It expresses your personality just as your clothes and speech do.

WHAT TO DO ABOUT GLOVES

"When you are being introduced to someone and have on gloves, should you excuse yourself or not mention it?"

"What does a man do under these conditions, if he is wearing gloves: (a) He is introduced to another man on the street? (b) He is introduced to a woman in the lobby of a theater?"

Authorities differ markedly in their pronouncements as to what is proper to do about gloves in handshaking. This difference of opinion gives you more leeway to follow your own inclination than might otherwise be the case. One thing is certain, however, and that is that it is considered better to go ahead and shake hands with your gloves on than it is to keep someone waiting with an outstretched hand while you fumble awkwardly to pull one glove off. Better to go ahead, shake hands, and not mention the glove than to give undue emphasis to it either by struggling to get it off or by speaking about it. But man or woman, if you want to take your glove off to shake hands and can get it done inconspicuously, you are certainly free to do so, Emily Post notwithstanding. Many people who qualify as ladies and gentlemen do prefer to remove the right glove for handshaking as a mark of sincerity and respect for the other person.

TAKING LEAVE AFTER AN INTRODUCTION

"What is the proper procedure in leaving a group, some of whom you have just met?"

"When you have just been introduced to a group, are you supposed to excuse yourself if you are going to leave?"

"Does a woman say 'I'm glad to have met you' when she is leaving?"

"What do you say when someone says, 'I'm glad to have met you'?"

After you have been introduced to a group of people it is impolite to leave immediately, without exchanging a few words of conversation. If you have been talking for some time, it is necessary only to say, "Good-by." You may also add, "I'm very glad to have met you." If you are called away or feel that you must leave hurriedly, you would say, "Please excuse me." You would not say good-by to the entire group, individually. One good-by is sufficient. If you are talking with an elderly person, man or woman, you should wait a reasonable length of time for the older person to terminate the conversation.

Either a man or a woman who is taking leave may say, to someone he or she has just met, "I'm very glad to have met you." The reply is "Thank you" or "Thank you very much" or "I'm glad to have met *you*."

FORGETTING NAMES

The memories of the younger generation for names are no better than those of their elders, if one may judge by the number of questions such as these:

"How can I best cover up my embarrassment in introducing someone whose name I've forgotten but should know?"

"I am talking with a person whose name I have momentarily forgotten. A third person, whom I know, joins the group. Should I attempt an introduction?"

"May one reintroduce himself to someone who has forgotten him?"

The ability to remember names is undeniably a great advantage to anyone who deals with people. We are pleased when someone whom we do not expect to know our name remembers it and pronounces it correctly. We feel deflated when a friend or acquaintance fails to remember it. Probably one reason why most of us forget names so readily is that it does not seem sufficiently important to us to remember them.

The first essential of remembering names is the genuine desire to do so and the willingness to make the necessary effort. It is important to get the person's name correctly at once. It sometimes helps to

1. repeat the person's name at the time you are introduced to him
2. ask him to spell his name if it is difficult
3. get some facts about him, such as the place where he lives or that he paints at Gloucester in the summertime or knows your best friend at Stanford or is interested in stamp collecting.

Dr. Mursell in his book *Streamline Your Mind* suggests that when you are walking home after having been introduced to Mr. Robinson you look at a telegraph pole and murmur to it, "How do you do, Mr. Robinson?" and imagine its look of pleasure at your recalling its name so well.

These suggestions may aid you, but there is no magic formula so far as we know that will prevent you from being caught in situations in which an introduction appears necessary and you cannot remember one person's name. Sometimes if you see that such a situation is about to arise, you can avert the difficulty by getting the information quickly from another person. Otherwise, there is nothing to be done except to say, "I'm very sorry, but I can't remember your name at the moment," whereupon the other person should give his name immediately. An experienced person, recognizing your embarrassment, will supply his name without waiting to be asked for it.

Mr. Hesketh Pearson in *Thinking It Over* tells the following incident of how one man met an embarrassing situation caused by forgetting the name of one of his guests. "A stranger and I had been waiting some time for Sir Herbert Beerbohm Tree at His Majesty's Theatre. Finally he came in and flung himself into a chair between us. 'Consider yourselves introduced,' said he, looking at the ceiling, 'because I remember only one of your names, and that wouldn't be fair to the other.' "

When another person has obviously forgotten not only your name but you, you may reintroduce yourself if you do it courteously and may suggest the time and place of the last meeting: "I am James Surrey. I believe that I met you at the country club dance last Friday night."

WHEN ARE INTRODUCTIONS NECESSARY?

Does one introduce or not on such occasions as the following:

"If one meets other friends on the street or at a public dance, is it necessary to introduce one's escort, if the friends seem disposed to talk?"

"At a houseparty should one introduce his guest to all the other guests, even though there are many and he feels that she is not particularly interested in meeting everyone?"

"Should you introduce your date to the chaperons at a dance?"

The principal point to remember in this connection is that a well-bred person does not intentionally offend another person. It is better to err on the side of making too many introductions than to offend someone by not introducing him.

You should always introduce

1. any guest whom you bring into your home to all other members of the family
2. all guests to the guest of honor
3. all guests at a houseparty
4. dinner partners, and all guests at one table
5. members of any small group
6. your partner to the chaperons at a dance, unless the dance is one involving several hundred couples. At such affairs, you should do so if you are a member of any committee or in any other way have responsibility for the affair
7. all players in any game involving a few players, such as bridge, tennis, or badminton
8. the visiting guest to the hostess who has included him in her invitation.

Usually it is not necessary to make introductions on the street. If a person whom you know stops for a moment to talk with you, your companion may easily walk on a few steps and wait for you. If you invite the third person to join you, you will, of course, introduce him to your companion. He should not join you without invitation. At a dance, public or private, you are expected to introduce the friends who come up to speak to you.

WHAT TO DO IF NOT INTRODUCED

Have you ever been uncertain of the correct procedure in one of the following situations?

"What do you do if someone joins your party and no one introduces you?"

"If one couple meets another couple and the boys, who are acquainted with one another, do not introduce the girls, should the girls speak to each other?"

"What should you do if you are attending an informal reception for a visiting celebrity and no one introduces you?"

All of us know that it is a most embarrassing situation to be with a small group of people and not know who several members of the group are. The most uncomfortable thing you can do is to let the situation continue. Ask your partner or someone else in the group whom you know to introduce you. If for some reason you find yourself face to face with a stranger, with no one to introduce you, introduce yourself: "I'm Martha Brown. I don't believe I've met you." If you meet another couple and do not know the other girl (or boy), suggest to your partner that he introduce you.

If the person that you think you have not met thinks that he has met you before, it is probably better not to make an issue of the matter, but to dispose of it as lightly as possible. You can always say that you have the worst memory in the world so please to help you out. If you are a really experienced and considerate person, you will never put another person on the spot deliberately by letting him flounder around trying to remember your name or badger him with "You don't remember who I am, do you?"

It is not necessary to meet everyone at a large function, but it is important to meet the guest of honor. After you have stood around first on one foot and then on the other for several minutes waiting to be introduced, it is perfectly acceptable to ask someone whom you know to introduce you. You may introduce yourself, but it is less awkward to be introduced by another person.

THE INTRODUCTION OF COUPLES

Probably there is no one type of introduction that young people are called upon to make more frequently than that of introducing their companion for the evening to other friends who also have a date. A few general principles may be borne in mind. In introductions between couples, it does not matter greatly who takes the initiative, *just so someone does.* Usually the person, man or woman, who knows the largest number of persons in the group will begin the introductions. The same general principles hold for introductions between couples as between individuals. The men are introduced to the women. It is customary when making an introduction between two men or between two women to show courtesy to your companion and introduce another man to your escort, another girl to your partner.

Let us suppose that two couples meet at a dance. A very common situation is that in which the girls know each other and the men know each other, but no one of them knows all in the group. The couples are, we shall say,

John and Mary
Jim and Susie

It doesn't matter whose social conscience moves him first, for the general rules governing introductions hold. Suppose John took the initiative.

John: Mary, I see you girls know each other. This is Jim Hunter. Jim, Mary Brown.

Jim would then take over.

Jim: And this is Susie Campbell—John Marshall.

Or if the girls did not know each other it might be:

John: Mary, this is Jim Hunter. Jim, Mary Brown.

Jim: And this is Susie Campbell—Mary Brown, John Marshall.

After all, the important thing is that everyone should be identified so he or she will feel a part of the group, so it isn't too important who does what, if the purpose is accomplished.

INTRODUCTIONS TO A GROUP

Many times, one is called upon to introduce a friend to a group of men and women to whom he is quite unknown. Some of the difficulties that may arise in such a situation are:

> *"How do you introduce a man or a girl or both to a mixed group?"*
>
> *"In introducing a group of people, do you have to introduce each person individually, or can you introduce the group?"*
>
> *"How does a hostess introduce a guest to a roomful of people? Does the guest acknowledge each introduction?"*
>
> *"When attending a club function, should a man attempt to introduce his date to everyone or to only a few in the group?"*

The introduction of one or more individuals to a group is complicated at best. The smoothest procedure is to mention the guest's name first and then the name of each person in the group in turn just as they happen to be standing or sitting. "I should like to introduce my guest Mr. Wilson—Miss Brown, Mr. Burton, Miss Girton, Mr. Turner." In informal introductions, the hostess might say, "I should like to introduce my guest Bill Wilson—Mary Brown, Joe Burton," and so on. The guest acknowledges each introduction. A man shakes hands with the men to whom he is introduced unless circumstances make it awkward for him to do so. A woman simply bows in acknowledgment of each introduction. If the guests were a man and his wife, the hostess would say, "I should like to introduce my guests Mr. and Mrs. Wilson." The hostess would not introduce her guests to an entire roomful of people, because it is embarrassing to the guests, but rather to small groups at a time. At a tea or reception, the guests of honor might be in the receiving line with the hostess and would meet people in that way.

At a club function, it is not necessary to introduce one's partner to everyone present. You should introduce him to your special friends and to anyone else whom he expresses a desire to meet.

INTRODUCTIONS OF RELATIVES

"How should you introduce a friend to a woman who has recently married into the family?"

In general, members of the immediate family are not called by Mr., Mrs., or Miss in introductions, unless not to do so would confuse the person being introduced. They are referred to as "my sister," "my father," "my husband." "Mary, this is Bill Smith, who is going to camp with me this summer. Bill, this is Dick's wife." Mary answers, "How-do-you-do?" or "How-do-you-do, Bill?" and Bill replies, "How-do-you-do, Mrs. Burns?" or "How-do-you-do, Mary?" depending upon the degree of his familiarity with the family. Or, if a woman were being introduced, the form might be, "Mrs. Smith, have you met my sister-in-law Mrs. Julian?" If the father uses a special title, his son or daughter would say, "This is my father, Doctor [Judge] Julian," in order that the newcomer could use the title in addressing him.

*"When introducing your mother, who has remarried, do you
mention her present name?"*

Yes; otherwise the person meeting her would assume it to be
the same as your own and might make an embarrassing error.

"Whom do you introduce first, your girl friend or your sister?"

You might choose to make the introduction either way, depending on the circumstances.

"What is the proper way to introduce a divorced woman?"

Unless by special decree the court has restored to a divorced
woman her maiden name, she still carries her former husband's
surname and, in place of his Christian name, uses her own family name. Thus, Marjorie Wright, who has obtained a divorce
from John Ashton, becomes Mrs. Wright Ashton. She would
be introduced as Mrs. Ashton. If John Ashton had remarried,
and particularly if he and his present wife were at the same
social function with his former wife, discretion would indicate
introducing the first Mrs. Ashton as Mrs. Wright Ashton. If
she were using her maiden name, she would be introduced as
Miss Wright.

INTRODUCTION OF A GUEST

*"In introducing a guest to the hostess, should the guest always
be presented to the hostess, even though the hostess may be
younger than the guest?"*

Yes, unless your guest is a very distinguished person.

*"Should the person bringing a visitor to a party introduce the
visitor to each person or rather introduce him to the one giving the party, who will do the introducing?"*

You should not bring a visitor to a party unless arrangements
have been made in advance with the hostess. If you have re-

ceived her consent to bring a visitor, you should introduce him to the hostess at once and then to other friends whom you would like him to meet.

"When a girl wishes to introduce a boy to both her parents at the same time, how should she go about it?"

She might say, "Mother, this is John Standish [Mr. Standish], who is taking me to the dance tonight. Father, John Standish [Mr. Standish]."

"Is it absolutely incorrect to introduce people by their nicknames: Example: Jerry Emerson (girl)?"

No, not in informal introductions.

"If your name is mispronounced during an introduction, should you let the error go or correct it?"

If the introduction is a casual one and you do not expect to see the person again, you might very well not call attention to the error. If the correct pronunciation of your name is very dear to you, or if you expect to see the person again soon, you might say, "I'm sorry, but I think you misunderstood my name. It is Dirks, not Burkes."

"What do you do when you are introduced to someone whom you have just met?"

A situation of this kind could easily occur at a large tea or reception. Your cue is the light of recognition, or the lack of it, in the other person's face. If it is obvious that he remembers that he has just met you, you would say, "Yes, Mr. Brown and I have just been introduced," or "We have met each other before." If, however, the other person indicates by his expression and manner that he has no remembrance of having seen you before, the best thing to do is simply to say, "How-do-you-do?" even though it requires self-restraint.

"Is a married woman given preference over an unmarried woman in an introduction?"

There was a time when this distinction was rigidly adhered to. Now, however, the age distinction seems to be more important. When introducing two women of the same age, one married and one unmarried, you might say, "Mrs. Twenty-five, may I introduce Miss Twenty-four?" but you would say, "Miss Forty, may I introduce Mrs. Twenty-five?"

"How does one introduce a minister? Is he Mr. Carr, the Reverend Carr, or the Reverend Mr. Carr? How is a Catholic priest addressed in introductions?"

A Protestant clergyman is introduced as Mr. Burton, unless he holds the honorary title of doctor of divinity, in which case he is Dr. Burton, but he is *never* Reverend Burton. If you wish to identify him, you may say, "This is Mr. Burton, the pastor of the Hyde Park Presbyterian Church." A clergyman with the title of Bishop is introduced as Bishop Burton. If he is an Episcopal clergyman, you speak of him as the rector of the church, rather than the pastor. A Catholic priest is introduced as Father Burton.

"Are a doctor and a dentist given their titles in social introductions?"

Both a doctor and a dentist are given their professional titles in social introductions. Both are "Doctor Smith."

On Campus

Introductions involving faculty members are made more complicated by the necessity of addressing professors and other dignitaries by their correct titles. When there are deans, comptrollers, directors, doctors, professors, instructors, and assistants to be introduced, it is not surprising that students find themselves confused in such situations as the following:

"*In formal introductions, which of these forms is correct for introducing a college professor—Mister, Doctor, or Professor?*"

"*How do you introduce the President of the University and a visiting celebrity; the President and your mother and father; the President and a girl student?*"

"*In introducing your mother and a woman teacher about her age, which one is presented to the other?*"

"*Does one say, 'Professor Grey, this is Miss Burton,' or 'Miss Burton, this is Professor Grey'?*"

ACADEMIC TITLES

There are four types of title that you will encounter frequently on the campus: the academic, honorary, administrative, and instructional. Of the academic titles, the best known is that of doctor of philosophy, which, aside from the professional degrees, is the highest awarded for work in any academic field. This degree is commonly known as the Ph.D., and one who holds the degree is called "Doctor."

Among the honorary degrees are those of Doctor of Laws, Doctor of Divinity, Doctor of Science, Doctor of Literature, and Doctor of Letters. A holder of any one of these degrees is known as "Doctor." Neither the academic nor the honorary titles are dependent upon the position that the person holds in the institution with which he is connected.

The administrative and instructional titles are derived from the person's connection with the institution in which he is employed. Administrative titles are: president, chancellor, provost, dean, director, comptroller, and so on. The instructional titles are, in descending order: professor, associate professor, assistant professor, instructor, and assistant. A professor, associate professor, or assistant professor is given the title of "Professor."

Unless you happen to be associated with an institution that prides itself on using no titles, or unless you know that an individual prefers not to be addressed by title, an administrative officer or a professor should be given one of his titles in the classroom, in his office, on the street, and at college social functions. Which title is to be used is a matter of choice.

The President or Chancellor is usually addressed as "President Able" or "Chancellor Able." Deans are usually called by their administrative titles, but it is not incorrect to speak of Dean Black as Dr. Black or Professor Black, if he holds these titles. A person who is both a "Doctor" and a "Professor" may be addressed by either title. A teacher who holds a doctor's degree but does not have professorial rank is addressed as "Doctor." If he is an instructor without a doctor's degree, he is called "Mister."

Since the President is the official head of the University and his wife the "first lady" of the campus, they are in a class by themselves as far as introductions are concerned. You would introduce your mother and your father, a visiting celebrity, or a girl student to the President and to his wife. "How do you do, President Able? I am John Burton, a junior in Chemical Engineering. May I introduce my mother and father?" If the parents' surname is different from the student's, he should indicate it in the introduction by giving their name. You will note that the introduction of your mother to the President of the University is an exception to the rule "Introduce the man to the woman." In introducing a celebrity to the President, you would say, "President Able, this is Mr. World Famous."

In introducing your mother and a man professor or your father and a woman professor, you would follow the general rule of introducing a man to a woman and present the man professor to your mother: "Mother, this is Professor Grey—my mother, Mrs. Burton"; but you would introduce your father to a woman professor: "Professor Brown, may I introduce my father, Mr. Burton?" In introducing your mother and a woman professor, or your father and a man professor, the order of the introduction is optional. In most social situations you would probably show deference to your mother and father and would, therefore, introduce the woman professor to your mother and the man professor to your father.

If as a woman or man student you or you and your residence group were entertaining a professor or a professor and his wife in your house, you would invariably mention the professor's name first in introducing your housemates.

"Professor Smith, this is Mary Kenton, my roommate."

"Professor and Mrs. Smith, these are some of the men on our corridor—John Masters, Leo Burke, Charley Moses, and so on."

In introducing your housemother, you would say "Mother Mac, (or whatever you normally call her) this is Professor Smith from the English Department—Mrs. McDougle, our housemother." This would hold whether Professor Smith were a man or a woman.

INTRODUCING YOURSELF

It is practically mandatory to introduce yourself to members of the faculty at any social function for which you have any responsibility and is a courtesy that is always in order at any social affair. The form may be simply, "How do you do, Professor Grey? I am John Smith. I am in your eight o'clock chemistry class." Such a gesture is greatly appreciated by harassed faculty members who may be vainly trying to remember where they have seen you before.

"Does being in class with another person serve as an introduction?"

In small schools, being a student in the same college serves as sufficient introduction for a greeting on the street or for conversation. In large schools, being a member of the same class (unless it is a large lecture section of several hundred students), laboratory section, or residence unit serves the same purpose. If you are in doubt, it is much better to speak and be friendly than to ignore the other person.

It is not necessary for a girl to introduce her escort to all the girls or to all the couples who happen to be in the living room of her residence unit when he calls. An introduction to one or two couples is sufficient. *She should, however, introduce him to the housemother, since the latter is the official hostess.* After the first introduction, the man should speak to the housemother when he calls again and should introduce himself to her for several times until he is sure that she knows his name. A man who invites a girl to his fraternity house for dinner should always introduce his guest to the faculty sponsor, housemother, or head of the house.

At a house dance, you are always expected to speak to the chaperons and guests of honor and to introduce your companion. Probably no one command of courtesy is more widely ignored than this one. It may be said that chaperoning at a dance is a great bore unless students do make an effort to greet the chaperons. Probably the fact that students are careless about speaking to the chaperons and about making them feel welcome causes more adults to refuse to chaperon college dances than any fear that they may have to deal with an unpleasant social situation. Even chaperons are human!

In exchange dinners, tea dances, and other such affairs at which one group of students entertains another, the initiative in introductions should be taken by the men when the affair is in their house and by the girls when they are hostesses. When the men are hosts, they know practically all the men who are present at the affair, but the girls may know only their current partners. When the girls entertain, the situation is reversed, and the girls know one another, whereas the men may know only their own partners. In these instances, the respective hosts and hostesses should not hesitate to take the lead in making introductions.

The organization of a receiving line is discussed also on page 167. The duty of introducing guests to the first person in the line is an important one, however, as far as the smoothness of the affair is concerned. Someone who knows a great many of the guests should be detailed to the job. It is his responsibility then to know or to ask the name of each guest and to introduce him to the first person in line. It is obvious that it is important to speak the guest's name clearly and distinctly to the first person in line, for that person has the responsibility of introducing the guest to the next person in line. He must hear and understand exactly if he is to give the guest a fair chance to retain his own name by the time he reaches the end of the line.

For any public reception in connection with a community project or business or professional conference, as contrasted with a relatively private one held in someone's home or in a small group living unit, it is often found useful to supply the members of the receiving line with identifying, easily readable name tags. Celebrities standing in the line may be grouped in twos and then the twos separated by an interval of space. Guests going down the line may be instructed by the person who might usually have the job of starting the introductions to the line to introduce themselves to each small section in the line. This is easy if those in the line have on name tags. "President Howe, Mrs. Howe, I am John Bullett." Or if you and your date are going down the line together "President Howe, Mrs. Howe, this is Mary Gardner and I am John Bullett. We are both sophomores in the School of Science."

This procedure permits those in line to give full attention to each guest as he introduces himself without having to worry about making an introduction to the next celebrity in line.

Chapter Three

TECHNIQUES FOR THE TABLE

WHERE DO YOU PUT *your iced-tea spoon when no coaster is provided? your dinner knife and fork when you have finished the dinner course? your napkin when you are called to the telephone during dinner? your dinner knife and fork when you pass your plate for a second helping?*

WHAT WOULD YOU DO *if you found a fly in your dessert when you were dining at a friend's home? if you got a piece of gristle in your mouth which you couldn't chew or swallow? if you spilled jam on the tablecloth at a dinner party? if you came into the dining room late at your college residence hall?*

WOULD YOU *leave food on the floor in a cafeteria if you had spilled it? cut your head lettuce with your knife? put your napkin upon the table before everyone had finished? dip your napkin in your finger bowl? butter a whole slice of bread at once? break a hamburger sandwich in two before eating it? wait for the hostess at your table to begin eating before you started?*

THE VERY PLEASANT HABIT of eating three regular meals a day is wide in its range of social possibilities. One may vary it all the way from snatching a hamburger on the run, so to speak, to entertaining a world celebrity or the one man or girl in the world at a formal dinner. Traditionally, breaking bread together is a social occasion regardless of how simple or how elaborate the food and service are. From time immemorial, inviting one to share food has been regarded as the ultimate gesture of friendliness. Mealtime is the time for fellowship, the exchange of ideas, the cementing of friendships. It is because of this vitally important possibility of improving one's human relationships while dining that one needs to have the physical skills of the rite

at one's finger tips. Knowing what to do, and how to do it, so
well that it is habitual and automatic is the goal. Then, and
then only, can one's entire attention be turned to the social
issues, the human relationships, involved.

Although there are, perhaps, more minute rules in this area
of social behavior than in any other, there are still hundreds of
situations not covered by rules in which one will have to apply
to the best of his judgment the general principles of good taste,
inconspicuous action, and consideration for the sensibilities of
others. No one can possibly foresee all the things that may happen in connection with eating; too many people are busy thinking up new things to eat and new ways of serving old things.
Reasonable proficiency in the fundamental skills will build confidence in one's ability to meet the unusual situation with
equanimity. No layman should be too discouraged by an accident or an unforeseen difficulty, however, as even Emily Post
admits that she might spill jam on the tablecloth sometime.

Techniques for the Use of Silverware

The whole art of the use of silverware is based on knowing
how to hold the "fundamental implements" easily for their
most efficient use and knowing what to do with them when
you are not using them. Selection of the proper implement is
comparatively simple if, in general, you

1. follow the lead of your hostess,
2. use your silver in the order of its arrangement beginning with
   the outside piece, and
3. trust your own judgment as to the requirements of the food
   at hand.

For conveying food to the mouth, the fork or spoon is held
firmly in the right hand with the thumb and first two fingers—
prongs (or bowl) up. When eating semisolid foods, such as
cereal or ice cream, the spoon is dipped toward you and the food

taken from the end of it; but when eating soup, the spoon is dipped away, and the liquid sipped noiselessly from its side. While cutting with a knife, the fork is held in your left hand with the prongs downward and *the handle pressing into the palm of your hand.* Your index finger extends in a straight line down the handle. Your knife is held in your right hand in exactly the same manner. The index finger should not extend below the hilt of either the knife or fork. The knife cuts on the *outside* of the fork. Elbows must be kept in and low when you cut if you would appear skillful. The amount of food taken on either the fork or the spoon at any one time should represent just one bite. Nibbling at a bite of meat or licking off part of a spoonful of ice cream are definite violations of accepted usage.

CONTINENTAL AND AMERICAN STYLES

After you have cut off a bite of meat, you may transfer it to your mouth with the fork still in your left hand tines down; or you may cut off two or three bites, lay your knife on the upper edge of your plate (blade edge toward you), transfer the fork to your right hand, and continue as you would if you had not had to use your knife for cutting. The former style of eating is known as the Continental; the latter as the American. The knife should be used as sparingly as possible. All vegetables are manipulated with the fork, including any transferring of butter to them. Likewise, all foods soft or tender enough to be cut or broken with the edge of the fork are so eaten. When eating with the fork, the tines are held up, and the fork used shovel fashion, except for meat which must be impaled securely in order to guarantee its safe arrival. One item at a time on the fork is the rule. The knife, on the other hand, is used only for cutting necessary items such as meats and perhaps baked potato skins and for spreading butter and perhaps jam on bread—never for actual eating and never for pushing anything on to the fork.

At any time during the meal that you are not using your knife (after you have once picked it up and used it), it should be placed on the upper right edge of the plate, blade edge toward you. Whenever you lay the fork down, it should be with the tines up near the center of the plate and the handle coming out to the lower right-hand corner of the plate. After you have finished the food on your dinner plate, the knife joins the fork. It is placed just to the outside of the fork, blade in the center of the plate, edge toward you, handle out to the lower right edge of the plate.

Salad forks are left in the same relative position on the salad plates. Butter spreaders, once they have been used, are always placed on the bread and butter plate—blade in the center, edge toward you, handle out to lower right edge of plate.

Spoons, in general, are left on the plate used under the soup cup, sherbet dish, or saucedish; or on the saucer of the tea, coffee, or cocoa cup. If a flat soup plate is used the spoon may be left in it. Almost everyone is familiar, however, with certain informal situations in which no small plate is used under the saucedish or sherbet dish. Instances in point are the use of a saucedish for creamed vegetables, stewed tomatoes, or other vegetables that cannot be eaten satisfactorily with a fork and the placing of the sherbet cup containing the dessert of ice cream, stewed fruit, or chocolate pudding directly on the table along with the main course. The most satisfactory place in which to leave your spoon in these cases is on your lunch plate in a line along with your knife and fork. Avoid leaving your spoon in any place where it might easily be knocked out of a dish. No part of any piece of silver that has been used is ever allowed to touch the table again. It is probably superfluous to add that to play with or finger one's silver never adds to one's poise or look of self-assurance.

"Where are you supposed to put your fork when you get a second salad?"

"Do you try to take your silver off your plate when you pass it for a second helping?"

When you are to be served a second helping, your salad fork should be placed on your salad plate and your knife and fork on your dinner plate exactly as you would place them when you have finished eating.

"Should one eat creamed vegetables served in a side dish with a fork or spoon?"

The general rule for vegetables is to use a fork if at all feasible. Common sense, however, dictates that you shouldn't waste a good thin cream or butter sauce if you are lucky enough to have vegetables served to you in it. Use your teaspoon when necessary and leave it on your dinner plate when you have finished—not out in the little side dish, where it might fall out easily.

"May one never use a knife to open a roll even when it is inconvenient to break it because it is so hard?"

"Should jam or jelly be put on one's bread with one's knife or fork?"

"Is it correct to spread butter with a fork if no butter knife is given?"

As far as bread or a roll is concerned, a knife may be used only to spread—not to cut. A knife, however, must be used to spread your butter, jam, or jelly on your bit of bread. Use your fork for your jam or jelly only if you are eating it as an accompaniment to your meal—not as a spread for your bread. And use your fork for your butter only when you are putting it on vegetables. Cheese is an item that may be spread with a fork on your cracker if you are eating it with a salad for which you are using no knife.

"Is it ever permissible to eat cake with a spoon?"

"When ice cream and cake are served on the same plate along

*with coffee and you are given a fork and spoon, with which
do you eat the ice cream?"*

*"Should pie à la mode be eaten with a fork alone or a spoon and
a fork?"*

*"Is it permissible to use a spoon with a dessert such as straw-
berry shortcake if there is quite a bit of juice?"*

Usually cake is eaten with a fork. If at a tea party you find
yourself with a small cake, a cup of tea, and a teaspoon, in all
probability the spoon is meant for the tea. The hostess believes
the cake to be such that it can be eaten easily in your fingers. If
you find, however, that your hostess has miscalculated the hard-
ening time of the icing, in the absence of a fork you will have to
use your spoon.

When ice cream, cake, and a cup of coffee all appear on the
same plate, as they very often do for tea or for informal evening
refreshments, you will probably use your fork for your cake
and ice cream and your spoon only for your coffee.

If both spoons and forks are available to you for such desserts
as pie à la mode and strawberry shortcake, you are quite at liberty to use both. In the more formal situations, a dessert spoon
and dessert fork are both supplied with the dessert. In most
ordinary dining, however, only one utensil is supplied.

*"Where is the iced-tea spoon placed if there is no coaster pro-
vided?"*

*"When sherbet is served at a meal, should you use a spoon or
a fork? What should you do with the spoon, if you use a
spoon?"*

*"Where does one put his spoon after eating a sundae in a
public confectionery where they do not use service plates?"*

The problem of what to do with spoons when no plate is
provided for them is difficult, yet we all know that dining in

comparatively informal situations often calls for such a decision. One thing certain is that you do not want to lay a used spoon back on the dining table. If you have a salad or a bread and butter plate, your spoon may be laid on it so that it will be out of your way. If there is no other plate besides your main lunch or dinner plate, then lay your iced-tea spoon on the outer edge of it as much out of your way as possible. Don't place the bowl of the spoon on the plate in such a manner that it is necessary for the handle to trail off on to the table.

Use a fork for your sherbet if the consistency of the sherbet will permit. If it has melted and you have to use a spoon, then your choice of resting places is the bread and butter plate, salad plate, and dinner plate in order named.

What to do with spoons at a soda fountain or in any situation where there is no possible plate to put them on constitutes a choice between two unsatisfactory possibilities. You either have to leave your spoon in your soda glass or sundae dish or lay it on the table. Out of consideration for the boy or girl who is going to have to clear the table for the next customers, and because on the whole it is neater, even though awkward, the better choice would seem to be to leave it in the glass or dish.

"Is it proper to use one's hands when reaching for a slice of bread, or should one use one's fork?"

By all means help yourself to bread with your fingers, being very careful to touch only the slice or roll that you are taking. Never use your own fork or any of your own individual pieces of silver to help yourself from a common serving dish. It is possible that you may find yourself in a situation in which you can see clearly that you are expected, for instance, to use your own knife to help yourself to butter. The only thing to remember in that case is "When in Rome. . . ." Don't let your hostess see that you have noticed the omission.

This question brings up the general matter of the use of serving utensils. Dexterity in the use of the large serving instruments is a great advantage as far as one's poise is concerned at the table. You will no doubt often have occasion to use a serving fork and spoon together to serve yourself almost any food including vegetables, salads, meats, and desserts. Manipulating both the large spoon and large fork at the same time in one hand is an art mastered by only the most expert of professional servers! Most of us have to be content with managing the spoon with the right hand and the fork as an accessory balancing implement in the left for most dishes such as vegetables, salads, or desserts. For meat, the fork is used in the right hand and the spoon in the left as an accessory implement. A serving fork alone takes on the role of shovel.

"Should one put her knife on her plate when finished even though she hasn't used it?"

It is not at all necessary ever to pick up any piece of silver that you have not needed to use. Whoever clears the table should clear the surplus silver before serving the following course.

"When there are two forks of equal size, which one should one use first when beginning the meat course?"

"When there are two forks of the same size at one's place, no salad fork, should one be used for the main course and one for the salad?"

Unless a salad fork is provided, the salad is usually eaten with the same fork as is the main course. The second "dinner" fork is probably intended for the dessert. In choosing between the two forks, use the one on the outside first, following the general rule that silver is ordinarily placed so that you use the outside piece first and the others in order as they are arranged. In really formal service, of course, the dessert fork does not appear until the dessert is served.

NAPKINS

"How is a napkin used correctly? How held, used, disposed of?"

"Does the departing guest leave the napkin at the right or left of the plate?"

"If called from the table during dinner, what should one do with his napkin—leave it on the table or on his chair?"

"When sitting down to eat, should you place the napkin in your lap immediately or wait until the first course is brought in?"

"When is the proper time to lay one's napkin down at a dinner?"

"When is the proper time to use a napkin at the table?"

In the picking up and laying down of napkins, one follows the lead of the hostess, if there is one, most rigorously. The hostess will pick up her napkin, unfold it to one-half its full size, and spread it across her lap just as soon as she is settled at the table. You may follow her lead at once. Of course, if there is no hostess, you pick up your napkin as soon as you yourself are well seated at the table. The hostess will place her napkin in a semifolded state back on the table at the left of the plate only when *all* persons at the table have finished and she is ready to give the signal for leaving the table. And no one puts his napkin back on the table until the hostess has first put hers back, after which he replaces his in the same manner.

Use your napkin frequently enough to make sure that you never sit for very long with a crumb on your chin. Always use it before you take a drink from a glass so that you will not leave a mark on the glass and always after taking a drink of any beverage so that you won't leave traces of the milk or cocoa or whatever you have on your mouth. Don't make the mistake of using the napkin so much that it appears to be only a nervous gesture, but err on the side of using it too often rather than not often enough!

Avoid crumpling and crushing your napkin into a wad or soiling it any more than necessary. This means, of course, that you must avoid getting your fingers sticky or greasy in the first place if you possibly can. Don't forget that fruit juices stain linen dreadfully. And it might be added, as a reminder to feminine diners, that lipstick is also an offender in the matter of stains.

If you are called from the table, leave your napkin in a neat, semifolded condition (one-eighth size suggested for a large dinner napkin) at the left of your plate. In an increasing number of situations you may find yourself with a paper napkin rather than the traditional linen one. It serves all of the same purposes, of course, and is handled in the same way.

DISHES

The proper use of dishes causes far less concern than does the use of silver. There apparently aren't nearly so many things that can be done incorrectly. The secret lies in the fact probably that the general rule underlying the use of dishes is to do as little to them as you possibly can. For the most part, leave them where they are placed. Leave your dinner plate, salad plate, bread and butter plate, dessert dish, glass, and cup and saucer where you find them. Don't be tempted to reorganize by shoving your dinner plate away from you when you have finished so that you will have room to lay your folded arms on the table or by moving your salad plate nearer to you, when you are dining in a home situation and your hostess has set table herself. If you are in a very informal situation where the dessert has been placed on the table along with the main course, you may certainly move it closer to you when you are ready for it. Avoid shoving your used main course plate out into the middle of the table however. In no case be tempted to "stack" your salad plate or your dessert plate on top of your used main-course plate. It is far too unattractive for you to enjoy or to be pleasant for your table companions to have to look at.

The question is asked:

"Should you tip your soup plate in order to obtain the last spoonful?"

Here, again, the less moving you do the better. It is considered permissible to tip your plate but certainly not mandatory and probably not so desirable as being content with the soup that you can procure without tipping it.

"When drinking from a goblet, where do you hold the goblet?"

"What is the correct way to hold your cup while drinking coffee or tea?"

A goblet is held firmly between your thumb and fingers at the juncture of the top of the stem and the bottom of the flared part of the goblet. Avoid spreading your whole hand around the flared top part. The handle of your coffee or tea cup should be held firmly between your thumb and fingers—not hooked through with your index finger. Whenever you are holding a glass or cup, watch your little finger that it doesn't get crooked out by itself in an affected pose. Keep it in close with the others.

These questions come from a men's dining room:

"If you don't drink tea or coffee, should you turn your cup over or leave it as it is?"

"Is it proper to put your cigarette ashes and stubs on your cup or on your plate?"

If you do not care for beverage, simply indicate the fact by a slight shake of your head and a "no, thank you" to the waiter as he is about to serve you. Cigarette ashes or stubs in coffee cups or on plates are one thing that makes dishwashing just a bit worse than it need be. In any situation when smoking is acceptable at the table but no ash trays have been provided, ask the waiter to provide you with one. Don't impose upon the good nature of the person who is going to wash your dishes.

"Is it proper to take your place card and nut cup from a banquet table when you leave?"

You are quite at liberty to take your place card, nut or candy cup, or anything that is obviously an individual favor of the occasion. In fact, the hostess usually is pleased if you do show your appreciation of her good taste in selecting her place cards by wanting to keep yours as a memento of her party. Do be sure, however, that you are not taking any of the hostess' permanent equipment, such as the little place-card holders that are often used.

The mere mention of a finger bowl seems to strike panic in the hearts of some relatively experienced diners-out because it symbolizes to them Formality with a capital F. As a matter of fact, a finger bowl is, or could be, a great convenience in many instances and is simple enough to use so that it should disturb no one. Its chief advantage, of course, is that it helps you to keep fruit juice from staining your napkin.

A finger bowl may be brought to you after you have eaten fruit at any meal. In this case, you are expected to use it at once, dipping the tips of the fingers of one hand at a time and drying them on your napkin held below the surface of the table. You may touch your moistened fingers to your lips, if you need to, and then dry them with your napkin, but don't be tempted to moisten your napkin for further ablutions. Care should be taken not to stain the napkin with lipstick when drying your lips. In some instances, the finger bowl may be brought to you on the dessert plate with the dessert fork and spoon lying on the plate at either side. You are then expected to place the silver on the table and lift the bowl (with the doily if one is present) onto the table, placing it to your left, and use it after you have finished your dessert. If you do not feel the need of dipping your fingers into the water, you need not feel obligated to do so.

Techniques for Certain Foods

Questions of how to manage specific foods are by no means limited to the unusual items on menus. Rather do they cover almost every imaginable sort of food found on the American table. Apparently it is interesting and probably worth knowing how to manipulate a lobster or an artichoke dexterously, but it is positively vital for anyone to know what to do about bread and butter or potatoes and gravy!

"Is it a breach of etiquette not to break your bread into single bites?"

"If there are no butter plates, should the butter be placed on the salad plate or on the service plate?"

"How should one eat jelly? Spread on roll, eat with fork, or how?"

"Is it wrong to have bread in one hand while eating with the fork or spoon in the other?"

Break off enough bread or roll for one or two bites, and butter it as you need it, resting it against the edge of the bread and butter plate while you apply the butter. If no bread and butter plate is available, then use the edge of your regular dinner plate. Nothing will make you look like your young brother with his after-school lunch so much as holding a whole slice of buttered bread in your hands and eating neat half-moon-shaped bites from it! If perchance jam or jelly is available, you have a choice. You may put it next to your butter on your bread and butter plate (or your dinner plate if bread and butter plates are not being used) and add a bit of it to each small piece of bread with your knife as you butter your bread. Or you may choose to place the jam or jelly on your dinner plate as accompaniment to the meat and eat it with your fork.

Incidentally, if you've broken off only a small bit of bread as you need it, you would not be sitting with bread in one hand and fork in the other taking alternate bites of bread and the rest of your dinner. If you *need* a pusher—simply can't manage without one—then use a small crust of bread for the purpose. It is better than your fingers—which is as much as can be said for it.

"Is it wrong to put bread on the plate and put gravy on it?"

"If potatoes are not mashed before serving, is it proper to mash them on your plate and place gravy over them?"

The matter of bread and gravy is an open question. Technically, gravy belongs with the meat and not on bread, or on potatoes either. Practically, this is hard to follow; for no items appear more often in ordinary American diets than bread, mashed potatoes, and gravy. The combinations of bread-and-gravy and potatoes-and-gravy are almost inevitable. The answer is probably to discriminate between the places where you may and may not indulge your taste. A dinner with any degree of formality about it is not the place at which to indulge! Ordinarily, put a small ladle of gravy on one side of the meat, next to the potatoes. Under no circumstances push down the mound of mashed potatoes with the bottom of the gravy ladle before you empty the ladle. Try to be content with the arrangement of the food on your plate as it comes to you—if the potatoes are whole, let them stay whole, and cut off only a bite or so at a time with your fork.

And no matter how much you like gravy, don't float your entire dinner in it. If you are dining quite informally with a group and your table hostess suggests that in the privacy of your own table you all might have bread and gravy—well and good. But that's one place where you should be slow to take the initiative—let the head of the table decide the problem.

"Your hostess says, as she passes her own homemade biscuits, 'Take two, and butter them while they are hot.' Should one do so?"

Hot biscuits are the one exception to buttering only the amount of bread you are going to eat immediately. Do break them gently in two, and butter them at once, for in no other way will your hostess feel that you are quite doing justice to her handiwork. Under no circumstances cut them, as cutting will make them "sad," as our grandmothers used to say.

MEAT

"Should all the meat on your dinner plate be cut up at one time?"

"Does one ever 'spear' meat?"

"Is it proper, when taking a second helping of meat, to cut a portion in two on the platter?"

"When steaks are served on individual platters, such as a 'sizzling steak,' how should they be put on your own plate?"

"Should you put the catchup on the meat or 'dunk' the meat in the catchup?"

The problem of how much meat to cut up at one time really depends upon the "style" of eating that you prefer. You may follow the Continental method of cutting off one bite of meat at a time and conveying it directly to your mouth, with your fork remaining in your left hand, tines down, as it was for the cutting. Or you may prefer the American style of cutting off two or three bites of meat, laying down your knife, transferring your fork to your right hand, and eating the bites of meat interspersed among bites of the rest of your dinner. You would never cut up your entire serving of meat at one time and then eat it all straight away. It is granted that the Continental style is perhaps more efficient, and certainly to be preferred to a zigzag performance of transferring the fork for every single bite.

On the other hand, it is perhaps a little easier to appear leisurely and to give more attention to conversation if you follow the other procedure. Regardless of whether you elect the Continental or the American style, the meat is pierced with the tines of the fork in order to guarantee its safe transfer. When, however, you are helping yourself to a portion of meat from a platter with a serving fork, you slide the serving fork under the portion and balance it as dexterously as possible while transferring it to your own plate. You may and should cut a portion in two when taking a second helping, if you wish only a small one, *provided* you can do it with the serving implement or implements at hand. You may never use your own knife for the purpose.

If, on a separate platter, you are served a whole steak or a portion larger than would normally be put on your dinner plate, your cue is to cut off possibly a half or a third of it and transfer it to your own plate. Probably no large service implements will be furnished (except possibly a spoon), so you will use your own knife and fork for the cutting. You can then use your fork and whatever spoon is available to lift the cut portion to your own plate and to serve yourself with the accompanying gravy.

Catchup is admittedly hard to use without making your plate look untidy. Probably the best advice is to use it sparingly in any case. A cosmopolitan palate likes the distinctive flavors of meats; it doesn't like them all to taste alike, especially all like catchup! Since catchup is too thin to eat in separate bites as you would chili sauce, jelly, cranberry sauce, or pickle relish, the next best thing is to eat a small bit of it with a bite of meat. When helping yourself to catchup, place it at one side of your meat, and then transfer a little of it with your fork to each individual bite as you eat it.

POTATOES

"How should one eat French fried potatoes?"

"Should one eat short shoestring potatoes with a fork?"

"What is the correct procedure for removing potato chips from the serving dish to my plate, and how do I eat them once I get them?"

"What is the proper way to eat a baked potato?"

In many restaurants, French fried potatoes or shoestring potatoes are often served on the same platter as the steak or in a small service dish by themselves. Transfer them to your own plate by means of a spoon which you have used on the steak and gravy and your own fork, unless service implements are provided. They are eaten with your fork the same as most other vegetables. An exception might be made for potatoes that are crisp all the way through and cannot be cut with a fork without likelihood of their shooting off on to the table cloth or the floor. It would seem feasible to eat them with your fingers provided that you manage them daintily. Boys may object to the term "daintily," but the process has to be that to be justified!

If potato chips weren't so good, we should almost say that there should be a law limiting them to picnics, because they cause so much difficulty. Their popularity saves them, however! If you meet potato chips in a picnic situation, and they are without serving utensils, then take them with your fingers— a very few at a time, so that you don't touch any others in the bowl. If you find them on your lunch table or at a buffet supper and a large spoon and a large fork together provided as serving utensils, then try to use them. If there are no utensils, you are free to help yourself with your fingers. Once you have the potato chips on your own plate, there is no feasible way of eating them except with your fingers.

The usual way of eating a baked potato, either white or sweet, is to break it open with your fingers or with your fingers and fork; mix the butter, salt, and pepper into a third or fourth of it at a time with your fork as you need it. The things that you may not do are to scoop out the insides with your knife or apply your butter with your knife. Whatever scooping and buttering are to be done *must* be done with your fork. Remember that the baked skin is good for you dietetically and considered a choice morsel by many, so do not hesitate to eat it too. If you need to use your knife to cut the skin, by all means do so, but often the whole procedure may be managed by a fork alone.

FINGER FOODS

"What, specifically, are the foods one may eat with the fingers?"

"Is it permissible to eat chicken on the bone or mock chicken legs by picking them up with the fingers?"

"Is it proper to eat bacon with the fingers?"

"Is it proper to pick up a meat bone and eat from it at the table?"

"Is it improper for one to pick a pickle up with one's fingers?"

Any foods that can be eaten neatly without getting the fingers sticky or greasy may be treated as finger foods. Any foods that will adhere to your fingers at all and consequently soil your napkin are definitely "out" as finger foods. Possible classification: Finger foods—olives, nuts, whole pickles, celery, radishes, and other raw vegetables served as relishes; small fresh fruits, such as plums, cherries, grapes, whole strawberries; or larger fresh fruits, such as bananas, or those which are not too juicy to quarter, pare, and handle in the fingers, such as apples and pears; breads, crackers, sandwiches, candies, cookies, non-sticky cake, dry crisp bacon, potato chips and dry crisp shoe-string potatoes, and corn on the cob.

Fried chicken, at a picnic, may be eaten in the fingers, provided always that you do it in such a way as not to appear ravenous and that you have an adequate supply of paper napkins at your disposal. Very dry, crisp bacon might be eaten with your fingers As for chop bones, "mock or city chicken legs," fish, or fried chicken, at the table with other persons present, you will do better to be content with the portion you can procure with your knife and fork.

"What is the correct way to eat a soft-boiled or hard-boiled egg?"

"How is sweet corn on the cob supposed to be eaten so as to be correct?"

"The correct way of eating artichokes puzzles me."

Egg cups that hold the soft-boiled egg in place while one eats it from the shell are seldom used in this country. Our usual custom is to turn the egg out into a cup and add butter, salt, and pepper to taste. This operation neatly done requires some skill. Cut the shell with a quick, sharp blow of your knife, if possible without cutting through to the yolk. Then break the halves gently apart with your fingers, letting the part of the egg that will, drop into the cup. Scoop the remainder out with the teaspoon with which you are going to eat the egg once it is ready. Transfer the butter which you are putting into your egg from your bread and butter plate or breakfast plate to the edge of the egg cup with your fork or your knife. Stir it into the egg with your spoon.

If hard-boiled eggs are tapped gently, their shells usually shell off more easily than if they are hit hard. Anywhere that a hard-boiled egg in its shell is served to you, you may certainly eat it in your fingers. If the egg is served to you as part of a salad, then, of course, you would use your fork for it. If it is served as a deviled egg, perhaps with such other relishes as celery and olives, it is eaten with the fingers.

Corn on the cob rates high in palatability, low in ease of handling. It is hard enough at best to retain one's dignity while eating corn on the cob, but it can be done. If the ear is large, break it in half with your fingers so that you can manage the piece with one hand. Butter and salt only a small portion of it at one time, using your knife to apply the butter. Then chew softly.

Artichokes are not nearly so forbidding as they first look. Pull the leaves off one or two at a time with your fingers, dip in the melted butter or sauce provided, and eat the soft palatable end. Stack the leaves neatly on the side of your plate as you finish each one. When you have pulled off all the leaves, hold the remainder solidly on your plate with your fork, cut away the thistle part with your knife, trim the edges, and eat the heart with your fork.

SOUP

Most persons seem fairly certain regarding the often emphasized major soup techniques, such as dipping toward the outer edge of the dish, dipping up only scant spoonfuls instead of brimming ones, and sipping noiselessly from the side of the spoon. Questions regarding this popular item of diet run along somewhat different yet important lines.

"When served soup that is too hot to eat immediately, what should one do?"

"Is it improper to blow on your soup?"

"Is it proper to drink one's soup when served conveniently?"

"Is it permissible to put oyster crackers in your soup?"

"When eating soup with crackers, does one replace the spoon in the bowl while taking a bite of cracker? Does one replace the cracker on the plate while using the spoon?"

Remember that "hot soup *hot*" is the goal of any cook worth her salt. You wouldn't like it if it were lukewarm when you got it. Take time to eat your soup in a leisurely manner—scant, half spoonfuls at a time dipped from the surface don't scald your tongue. Don't blow! Yes, you may drink your soup *if* it is conveniently served in a cup with one or two handles and if it is of a consistency that warrants drinking. Drinking is dependent, however, upon both of the afore-mentioned contingencies; so drink only after deliberation.

CRACKERS

Oyster crackers and small croutons may be dropped from your individual supply on your bread and butter plate or on your service plate into soup two or three at a time and then eaten. Large crackers or melba toast are also placed on your bread and butter plate or on the service plate under the soup container if no bread and butter plate is being used. These are broken off bit by bit as you eat them, so there should be no question of replacing the cracker on the plate while using the spoon. You may very easily have a bit of cracker in one hand and your spoon in the other momentarily. The thing to avoid in any case is using both hands at once so continuously and so energetically that you look as if you couldn't get your food fast enough to be happy. Between times of using your spoon and when you have finished your soup from a cup, place the spoon on the little service plate that is just under the soup cup. If a flat soup plate has been used, you may leave the spoon in the soup plate, if there seems to be too little room on the service plate for it.

SANDWICHES

An Englishman may have invented the sandwich, but the avid consumption of it by Americans has probably endowed it with an importance little dreamed of by the original nobleman. Sandwiches appear in amazing variety in a wide range of social situations—everything from the tiny open-faced tea sandwich of the sophisticated tea party to the tremendous whole-meal triple deckers of the sandwich shops and the traditional hamburger or wiener and bun of the best picnics.

"In eating a sandwich must it be broken up before one commences eating it?"

"What is the proper procedure in eating a three-decker sandwich? Dismantle it?"

"Is it impolite to leave bread crusts from sandwiches?"

"When we are served cold meat and bread, is it permissible to make sandwiches?"

"If hot dogs and buns are served separately, is it proper to put the hot dog in the bun?"

Probably the best general advice on sandwiches is to be neat and don't ever let yourself look greedy. Tiny sandwiches of three or four bites certainly do not need to be broken or cut into smaller portions; but all other sandwiches, including wieners and hamburgers, any place but at a picnic, should be. Break any sandwich that will break easily; otherwise cut it with your knife while you steady it with the fingers of your free hand. Cut it into small enough pieces that you can hold in *one* hand. The "triple decker" is unquestionably hard to manage; but if by cutting it into quarters or sixths and holding the layers tightly together, you can manage it in your fingers, by all means do so. You are at liberty to use a knife and fork on any elaborate sandwich that is more easily managed that way.

The pride of any good sandwich maker is to spread the butter and the filling out to the edges of the bread, so that the crusts will be a satisfying part of the sandwich. If the maker has done this, then do your part by eating the crusts. You can't reasonably be expected to eat too many dry crusts, but do what you can.

If appropriate sandwich materials, such as cold sliced meat, peanut butter, or cream cheese are provided, and you wish to combine them into a sandwich, there seems little reason why you should not. In a private home, you would certainly follow the lead and suggestion of your hostess; in a school dining room, it should be safe to ask permission of the head of the table to initiate the combination yourself, if he shows no inclination to do so; and if you are in an informal situation with no official hostess, you may certainly suit yourself so long as you do a neat job of it.

"Should I or should I not eat the lettuce leaf under my salad at dinner?"

"Is it permissible to cut a head-lettuce salad with a knife?"

"What does one do with relishes when passed to him—on which plate does he put them?"

"When a salt dish isn't supplied, where is the proper place for salt to be used for celery and radishes?"

"What is the best way to eat celery?"

"What is the proper way to eat an olive?"

"When an olive is served on a toothpick, as at a buffet dinner, is it taken off the toothpick, or do you eat it off the toothpick?"

The practice of not eating the lettuce leaf has almost completely faded out with the advent of the knowledge of vitamins. Formerly, in some circles at least, the lettuce leaf was looked upon merely as a decorative feature of the salad, whereas now it is recognized for its true worth. Do eat your lettuce! Not to do so gives you away one way or another—either you have a food dislike, which no cosmopolitan palate admits, or you are behind in your homework on dietetics.

SALAD

Indeed, it is permissible to cut a head-lettuce salad, the afore-mentioned lettuce leaf, or anything else that needs cutting. Cut what you can cut safely with your fork, but don't hesitate to use your knife rather than take a chance on all or part of the salad's shooting off on to the table. The obvious thing to avoid, of course, is cutting up more than a small portion at a time and so making your plate appear untidy.

What you may do with relishes is necessarily dependent upon the places available for them. The general rule is that *relishes are located according to the way they are to be eaten or according to the food that they are to accompany.* Anything that you ex-pect to eat with your dinner fork, along with your meat and vegetables, goes on your dinner plate. Such things as pickle relish, sliced or chopped pickles, spiced fruits, jams, jellies, cottage cheese, and so on would generally come in this group. Radishes, olives, whole pickles, celery—anything that you are going to eat with your fingers—may be put on your bread and butter plate, if one is being used. If this plate is not available, then use your salad plate if you have one, or, if neither of the smaller plates is available, then, of course, use your dinner plate.

The salt for celery or radishes may be put on the same plate with them—wherever that may be. Even though there may seem to be no good place on any plate for your salt, don't be tempted to put it on the table cloth! One of a good cook's am-bitions is to season food exactly to the diner's taste. Do her the honor of tasting your food before you salt it.

CELERY, OLIVES

If your piece of celery is long, break it into two- or three-bite lengths. Don't ever be caught with too big a piece of anything.

Only very tiny olives are popped into the mouth whole. An ordinary-sized stuffed olive is bitten in two, and an ordinary-sized ripe or green olive is eaten in two or three bites. Hold the olive in your fingers, and bite the meat from the pit. Thus you will have the pit in your fingers when you finish and won't have the problem of removing it from your mouth. Unless the olive on the end of the toothpick is one of these afore-mentioned tiny ones which may with propriety be taken in one bite, then it would seem wise to remove it from the toothpick and eat it in the ordinary way. There's no point in trying to nibble at it from the end of a toothpick.

FRUIT

> *"If fresh grapes are served for breakfast, how are they to be eaten—peeled or not? What about the seeds?"*
>
> *"Should a person attempt to eat the fruit in a cocktail or fruit drink?"*
>
> *"Is it all right if you touch your grapefruit with your left hand to help get the sections on to your spoon?"*

Fresh grapes are eaten one at a time with the fingers. If you are helping yourself from a serving bowl, do take a section of a bunch. Don't annoy your dining companions by pulling off one grape at a time as you need it. Remove the seeds and the skin, if you do not care to eat it, from your mouth with your fingers. Fresh cherries are eaten the same way, and their pits disposed of similarly. You may remove the pits of canned cherries from your mouth by dropping them into your spoon or into your fingers, whichever way you choose. The seeds of canned plums, peaches, or of any large fruit should never be taken into your mouth. Be content with whatever fruit you can cut from the seeds with your spoon.

Hold apples, pears, peaches, oranges, apricots, etc., in your fingers while you peel and quarter them. (Some people find it easier to quarter them first.) If the fruit is comparatively dry and solid, as in the case of apples and pears, you may pick up the quarters in your fingers and eat them. If they are juicy, as peaches are apt to be, then use your fork to eat them. Remember that it is only at picnics that you may pick up a whole fruit and bite into it. Oranges, of course, may be cut in half and eaten with a spoon if you like. Bananas may be peeled down a little at a time, and small pieces broken off with the fingers and eaten. If you are going to eat the banana sliced with cream, then peel all but a small portion at the end which you may use to hold on to—put the peeled end into the dish, and slice it downward gently.

The fruit in a cocktail or fruit drink is always tempting. It may certainly be eaten if you can get it without too much difficulty and eat it gracefully after you have it. You are always at liberty to tilt the glass after you have drunk the liquid and let the cherry or olive roll out or to pick up the cherry, olive, or slice of orange in your fingers, if you can reach it, after you have drunk all the liquid. The thing you may not do is to fish around for it before you have disposed of the liquid.

There is no reason why you should hesitate to steady your grapefruit with your left hand when you need to. In preparing grapefruit, it is difficult to separate all the sections completely. Understand how a grapefruit is put together, and use your spoon skillfully to remove the sections from their moorings. Don't try to cut through the tough white tissue. You can really avoid a lot of "squirting" by steadying your fruit and knowing where to use your spoon. Do not squeeze a grapefruit to get more juice.

FINGER BOWLS

Finger bowls are probably a greater help in connection with fruit than at any other time. If one is made available to you, by all means use it. Dabble the fingers of one hand at a time lightly in the water, and dry them on your napkin held in your lap.

Fruit juice stains linen napkins, so be as careful of them as possible. Probably, however, in the majority of instances, finger bowls will not be available to you, so it is your responsibility to manage your fruit so expertly that you will not get juice on your fingers.

SHRIMP, OYSTERS, LOBSTER

"Should shrimp be eaten whole? If so, how?"

"What is the correct way to eat lobster? Is it permissible to pick up lobster claws?"

"How are oysters eaten when they are served as a cocktail?"

"What is the proper thing to do if you get a fishbone in your mouth?"

Shrimp need not be eaten whole. In a cocktail, they are of such a consistency that they may be cut with the fork easily into convenient-sized bites. If they are boiled fresh and are served with their shells on, they are picked up in the fingers, shelled, dipped into the sauce, and bitten off as convenient.

Oysters, served raw as a cocktail, however, must be eaten whole. This is because of the unpleasant look of their insides. If a small container of cocktail sauce is served on the same plate with the oysters on the half shell, each oyster may be dipped into the sauce and then eaten. Managing lobster is not so difficult if it is well cracked. If you are unfamiliar with the technique of cracking one, by all means ask the waiter or waitress to crack yours for you. You may steady any part of the shell in your fingers that you need to in order to pick out the meat with the little fork provided. The claws may be pulled apart with the fingers. Unless you are very familiar with lobster, you should be content with the meat that you can secure with the fork.

Any fish may have an occasional small bone in it, no matter

how carefully it has been prepared. If you do get a fishbone in your mouth, the only thing to do is to remove it with your fingers as deftly as possible.

CAKES

"When small tea cakes are served without a fork, are they eaten with the spoon or picked up with the fingers?"

"Should one break hard cakes or cookies before one begins to eat them?"

"When you are served cakes in baking cups, do you eat them with your fork or take the cup off and eat the cake with your fingers?"

Very small cakes and cookies are eaten with the fingers. If no fork is served with the cakes, then it is certain that the person serving the food expects you to use your fingers, as no one ever plans deliberately to have cake eaten with a spoon. If the cake or cookie is larger than two or three bites, then it should be broken in two. If a cupcake is served in a paper baking cup, the stickiness of the icing determines very largely whether you remove the cup and eat the cake with your fingers or eat it from the cup with your fork.

If the icing on the cup cakes or any other cakes is soft and sticky, then take no chances with your fingers, but use your fork. If the cake is not sticky and may be broken, you may use your fingers if you wish.

NUTS

"Is it proper to eat nuts all through the meal when they are in individual nut cups?"

"If salted peanuts are served at lunch when only a dinner plate is used, are they put on the plate with the other food and eaten with the fingers?"

If nuts have been provided in individual nut cups, you may nibble at them whenever you like. If the dinner plate is the only plate available, by all means find a place on it for your salted peanuts, and eat them two or three at a time with your fingers. If a bread and butter plate is available and provides a better place for your nuts, then use it.

"Should cream and sugar be put in a demitasse?"

"How extensively should you stir and taste coffee or tea?"

"Is it proper to open your mouth wide and let the marshmallow slip in after you have finished your cocoa?"

"Is it ever proper to 'dunk'?"

"Does one take cube sugar from a bowl with one's fingers if there are no tongs provided? What about lemon?"

"What is the proper technique in handling a tea ball (bag) when it is removed from the cup?"

If sugar and cream are provided for your demitasse, then whether or not you use them is purely a matter of taste. Technically, however, you are not expected to need cream; so if it is not provided, do the best you can with the black coffee.

You may use your fingers with perfect propriety for lump sugar, whether or not tongs are available, provided always that you are meticulous about not touching any lump excepting the one to which you are helping yourself. A small fork is almost always provided for lemon; but if none is provided, then use your fingers carefully again.

Stir your coffee or tea the least possible; if it is iced, the same rule holds. To tinkle ice and fine glassware to the annoyance of other people at the table is very easy, so stir sparingly. Tasting of beverages may be done with the spoon, but you should not consume the whole cup of coffee or tea in that manner. Let one taste suffice.

Care should be taken especially on a diner, airplane, or boat not to fill the cup so full of cream that the least swaying motion will cause the beverage to spill over into the saucer. You should use your spoon to obtain the semisolid marshmallow in the bottom of your cup. Seeing just one person gulp his marshmallow will convince almost anyone of the undesirability of the habit! Avoid taking a drink of anything while you have food in your mouth and taking too large or too long a drink of water or any beverage no matter how thirsty you are.

A tea bag's only virtue is that it affords a handy way to make tea. As soon as your cup of water has become tea of the proper strength, remove the bag carefully, and place it on your saucer on the side nearest to you so that it will be as inconspicuous as possible. Since the wet discolored bag is no thing of beauty, don't be tempted to play with it and drip it around to your water glass and plate.

Dunking is an old custom, but it has never been a particularly attractive one to behold. Don't do it unless you are willing to put a severe strain on the tolerance of your dining companions.

EMERGENCY TECHNIQUES

"When one has an accident at the table, what is the best thing to do?"

"When something is spilled on the tablecloth, should an attempt be made to pick it up and place it on the plate?"

A serious accident, such as overturning a glass of water, immediately becomes the responsibility of the hostess. The offender should say sincerely and briefly, "I'm sorry." If the hostess has a maid at her disposal, she will immediately put the situation in her hands. If there is no one to turn to, she will repair the damages herself, assuring the unfortunate one that the matter is of no consequence. Fresh linen should be used for mopping up, and a fresh linen napkin spread over the damp or soiled area.

If, however, one has a minor accident, which does not require the help of the hostess, as, for instance, flipping a stray pea or a bit of salad on to the table or dropping a bit of jelly, then he repairs his own damage as inconspicuously as possible. He retrieves the bit of food with whatever implement he was using on it, plus the help of a small bit of dry bread or cracker, and places it on the side of the plate that it occupied originally. He does not eat this bit of food later. The important thing is to realize that anyone may be unfortunate and have an accident but that it is not a tragedy to be grieved over. Simply handle the matter as inconspicuously and neatly as possible.

"If at a dinner I drop my knife or fork on the floor, should I pick it up, or should I leave it on the floor?"

At a public formal dinner, there will be a waiter who should be aware of any such accident. If he does not notice what has happened, then tell him quietly as soon as you can get his attention, and ask him to bring you another fork. In any case where there is a hostess, she will in all probability see what has happened and take care of you. To which, of course, you would murmur an "I am sorry" and "Thank you very much." You would probably never have occasion to pick up the fork yourself at a formal dinner; but if the incident should occur when you are dining informally with friends and no servant were available, the situation would be quite different. Then you would retrieve the fork yourself and hand it to the hostess, who would exchange it for a clean one.

"If one accidentally drops some food in his lap, how should he unobtrusively care for it?"

If you have dropped food from your fork or spoon, you can only hope that it has landed on your napkin. Whether or not you have been lucky and it has hit the napkin instead of your lap, you should pick it up in the most convenient way. If it is dry and has not soiled your clothing, of course you can pick it up with your fingers, but a bit of gravy or vegetable will probably have to be retrieved with your fork or spoon. Remove the traces from your clothing with your napkin.

"If you drop some food on the floor of a cafeteria, should you try to clean it up, or should you disregard the matter?"

If you drop food on the floor of a cafeteria, or anywhere else for that matter, you should feel responsible for seeing that it is removed at once, before anyone has had the misfortune to step into it. In most situations, the person in charge of the dining room or a nearby waiter will observe what has happened and relieve you of responsibility in the matter. If, however, there seems to be no watchful employee at hand, you should pick up the food yourself, if it is such that you can handle it easily. If the situation is more serious, you should find the person in charge of the dining room and report your difficulty. Any manager with pride in his dining room will appreciate your cooperation in telling him of any situation that needs his attention.

"If you drop your napkin on the floor and the waiter doesn't notice, what do you do?"

How much you can help yourself is largely a matter of the position in which you find yourself. If you are in such a position that you can lean over easily and reach your napkin yourself, by all means do so. If, however, the napkin is beyond your reach unless you disturb those near you, then tell the hostess your predicament, and she will take care of you.

"When one finds a hair in the food, what should one do?"

This situation calls for great tact and tolerance. You simply must have enough confidence in those responsible for the food to know that no extraneous material is included in your food intentionally. If you have this experience in a private home or at a private dinner party, then you must be tactful enough to protect your hostess. Say nothing. Ignore the foreign material entirely. If you can hide the offensive bit from the gaze of your neighbors, do so. Eat only that part of the food on your plate that you care to eat. You can dawdle along so that you will not be conspicuous.

If, however, you have the experience in a public restaurant or somewhere else where you are paying for your meal and feel that you are entitled to one, you may take steps to remedy the matter, provided, always, that you do it courteously and tactfully. You may say very quietly to the waiter, "Will you please exchange my dinner plate for another one?" If he is a good waiter, he will take the plate without question, examine it carefully in the kitchen, and discover for himself why you wanted it changed. Tell him why you want it changed only if you have to. The thing you must not do in any circumstance is to talk about a hair or fly in the food or in any way call the attention of the other people at the table to the matter.

"Should a left-handed person attempt to eat with his right hand in order to try to avoid bumping the right-handed person on his left?"

"Is it correct for a left-handed person to reverse the positions of salads, desserts, etc.?"

"I am left-handed. When I put my knife and fork down naturally, it makes an awkward-looking plate. What should I do?"

A left-handed person is more or less handicapped if he is eating at a crowded table. If it is possible for him to procure a "corner" seat at the left end of the row, the situation is somewhat simplified. As for actually handling the silverware, placing it on the plate, and rearranging the position of salad or dessert, he should by all means make whatever adjustments he deems necessary, as the table has been set up for right-handed diners. His technique in any instance may be the reverse of that used by the other diners but will not be conspicuous if he is skillful.

"Supposing when you are eating that you chew something hard and can't swallow it. How should you dispose of the particle?"

The most acceptable way for removing anything from your mouth is with your fingers—thumb underneath and fingers above. In this way you can screen the particle from the sight of your neighbors as much as possible. It is at best an unsightly procedure to remove anything except fruit pits or a sliver of bone from your mouth. If, however, you do inadvertently get into your mouth an objectionable article such as a bad clam, bad oyster, bitter strawberry, or something that you definitely cannot handle with your fingers and yet cannot swallow, then remove it as inconspicuously as possible on the fork or spoon that you are using. Under no circumstances shield your mouth with your napkin while you dispose of the objectionable bit into it. The moral is, of course, to avoid the necessity of removing anything from your mouth if possible. A too hot bite must be swallowed once you have been so incautious as to take it into your mouth. Again discretion is the better part of valor!

"What can you do when a particle of food or a seed has lodged in an uncomfortable cavity?"

The answer is, unequivocally, that you must wait until you attain privacy before you can do anything about it! You will find toothpicks at the cashier's desk in all too many restaurants, but that fact does not justify anyone's ever using one in public. Certainly picking one's tooth with a finger, even though it is behind a napkin or running the tongue around and around the teeth in an effort to dislodge the offending particle is not a pleasant sight to others. Avoid offending those around you, even though it means that you may be uncomfortable for a few minutes yourself.

"What do you do if you strangle or get the hiccups at the table?"

"When called away from the table by a long-distance telephone call, do you excuse yourself and lay your napkin on the table or on the chair?"

The severity of coughing, strangling, or an attack of hiccups at the table has to guide you in your choice of action. If a swallow or so of water does not clear up the difficulty, then you will have to excuse yourself and leave the dining room as quickly and as quietly as possible. When you leave the dining room from a public dinner at a large table, excuse yourself to your immediate neighbors only. If you are at a private dinner, then excuse yourself to your hostess or the head of your table. Leave your napkin in a neat, semifolded condition at the left side of your plate.

ACCESSORY TECHNIQUES

Besides being familiar with the specific techniques of dining, there are certain accessory techniques important to your dining poise which you should probably remember.

If both men and women are present, then, of course, all the customary rules regarding the deference shown to women by men are in force. If, however, you are a young man or a young woman dining exclusively with members of your own sex, then remember that you may show deference to the older or more distinguished persons of the group or to guests by permitting them to precede you into and out of the dining room and assisting them to be seated at the table. A hostess, whether she be your mother in your own home, the mother of the household in which you are visiting, or the official hostess of any group dinner, is particularly entitled to the courtesy of having her chair held back for her by the nearest young person.

In many homes and in the dining rooms of many schools and camps, grace always precedes the meal. You will be wise to have this in mind so that you will not interrupt it inadvertently by conversation.

The way you sit in your chair determines very largely how you will appear to your dining companions. Most of us forget all too often how unprepossessing we look humped over, slouched down, or sprawled out in our chairs. A good position at the table involves

1. front edge of the chair seat just under the edge of the table
2. sitting erect
3. both feet flat on floor
4. hands in lap when not in use
5. leaning forward from the hips rather than humping over with shoulders.

The old question of elbows on the table is always present. Although accepted practice on this point is not nearly so strict as formerly, *it is still considered bad form to lean on the table while you are eating.* Perhaps between courses, during after-dinner conversation, or while dining with one or two persons at a small table in a restaurant where it is impossible to make yourself heard above the music without leaning forward, you could be permitted the elbows-on-table privilege. Don't ever make the possible exceptions to the general rule the excuse for half reclining on the table, however. And remember that what a famous personage may do in such matters without criticism is not necessarily a criterion for what the rest of us may do with propriety.

"Is it customary to wait until everyone is served before be-
ginning a meal?"
"Does one wait until the whole table is served beverages or
desserts before beginning his?"

It is generally considered courteous to wait until others have
been served, either at the beginning of a meal or at the beginning of a new course, before starting to eat. If there is anyone
acting in the capacity of a hostess, she should be the one to
begin eating and so to give the signal for others to start. At a
large banquet, it is considered acceptable to begin eating when
the persons in the immediate conversational group have been
served. A beverage may be drunk whenever it is served to you
during the meal, as everyone else will have something before
him either to eat or to drink and the situation is not the same
as if others were empty handed.

"Which hand should be used in passing food?"
"Is it proper to take food out of a dish if you are passing it to
someone who has asked for it?"

A dish that is being passed to you from the left would ordinarily be accepted in your right hand, transferred to your left,
and passed on. You should never help yourself from a dish someone else has asked you to pass without asking permission from
that person to do so. It would be far better if the person who has
asked you to pass the item would also take note of your needs
and ask you if you would care to help yourself.

Better still, perhaps, would be an awareness on your part of
the needs of your fellow diners which would prompt you to
ask if you might pass certain items within your reach before
they are asked for. In an informal situation where some dishes
are to be passed at the table, you are responsible for putting
into circulation the dishes nearest to you. These dishes should

always be passed to the hostess or head of the table first, if there is anyone at all acting in that capacity. In no case would you just pick up a dish and help yourself without offering it to the person nearest you first or reach for a dish that was nearer to someone else than to you.

CONVERSATION AT THE TABLE

From ages long past, the tradition has come to us that meeting together at the table is a time for sociability as well as for eating. Everyone is expected to throw off his own private worries and to exert himself to make the occasion a pleasant one for all present. Dinner is not the place at which to discuss the difficulty at the office, the failure on the chemistry test, or the quarrel with the neighbors. Above all, it is not the place to discourse on your food dislikes. If your mother or your hostess has prepared something that you particularly like, she will probably be pleased to have you mention it.

The conversation should be of such a nature that all can take part in it and enjoy it. Matters of exclusive interest to only one or two members of the group should be avoided. All such unpleasant topics as serious illnesses, operations, accidents, and embarrassing occurrences of any kind are better discussed elsewhere than at the table.

"Should you eat every morsel of food if you want it, or should you leave some on your plate?"

"Do you have to eat some of everything served to you?"

It is no longer considered necessary to leave anything on the plate. The thing to be avoided, however, is an overinterest in your food as shown by scraping of the plate or mopping it up with a crust of bread to obtain the last bit of food.

Being familiar with different and unusual foods is fun in itself, not to mention the fact that it might prove embarrassing to meet a new food for the first time in a situation where you would choose to be completely poised and at ease. People who have "been around" like almost all sorts of foods; they have cultivated a cosmopolitan taste. Don't miss the opportunity to educate your sense of taste along with your other educational activities.

Remember that all the somewhat unusual things are someone's prime favorites. Oysters, broccoli, liver, squash, fish, ripe olives, etc., all have their supporters who think that there is nothing like them. Remember how you are going to feel about a "man who is hard to cook for" because he doesn't like any of your favorites. And remember, too, that the enjoyment of the meal for a whole table may be spoiled by one person who doesn't like this or that. Silence is golden! You simply have to be able to eat items served to you by a personal hostess if you don't wish to offend her. And you never know when you will find yourself in a business or professional situation when you need to look as if you were completely familiar with everything that appears.

"How much water may you drink at one time?"

"Is it proper to take a drink of water as soon as you sit down at the table?"

Avoid taking a drink of water too soon after you are seated or drinking more than a sip or so of any beverage at one time. You can appear greedy by overeagerness in your water drinking as well as in your consumption of food.

"When one gets up from the table, is it proper to push the chair back under the table or to leave it in a random position?"

In most situations, it is better to replace your chair at the table. It will look neater; and if the dining room is crowded, it will help the flow of traffic. A woman is relieved of this duty, of course, by any man near at hand or by the waiter in a restaurant.

The College Dining Room

One may not generalize too much about college dining rooms, because each one has its own customs and traditions. There are, however, some general points that are applicable to most residence hall and organized house dining rooms. The smaller points of individual custom and tradition you will have to watch for carefully during your first few meals in the particular hall or house in which you find yourself. You will be able to pick these up easily and follow them accordingly if you are watching especially for them.

Attention to your personal appearance in preparation for a meal is essential, not only for the sake of your own poise and self-assurance but also for the sake of your housemates, who will enjoy you more if you are well groomed. The type of clothes that you will wear will be a matter of the tradition of the house. For breakfasts and lunches, you will probably wear the ordinary school clothes that you are wearing on the campus for the day, but you will doubtless have a shower and change into something different for dinner.

If, as a man student, you wear sweaters, T-shirts, and high-topped boots for your labs or wear athletic sweaters on the campus, you will probably change into an ordinary business suit with coat and tie for dinner. If you are one of the many girls who wear ankle socks and no stockings with sport shirts and skirts for the laboratory and classroom, you will want to have your shower and put on something not quite so informal for dinner. Any neat-looking dress or suit worn with ordinary stockings and shoes instead of the ankle socks and flat heels would be appropriate. Man or woman, it is not so much what you wear, as long as it is in general keeping with what the rest of the group is wearing, as the fact that you must look well groomed and meticulously clean as to face, hands, hair, nails, and clothes.

ENTERING AND LEAVING THE DINING ROOM

When a large group is to be served at one time, the matter of entering and leaving the dining room must be done skillfully if it is not to resemble a mild mob scene. Whoever is acting as head of the dining room, or whoever is the chief hostess in any situation, should be allowed to enter the dining room first. Whether or not you leave before all have finished will depend upon the custom of the dining room. Often, at breakfast or lunchtime, individuals may ask their table heads to excuse them as they finish, but at dinner everyone remains until all have finished. If this is the practice in your dining room, then be sure to show the head of the dining room the courtesy of letting him or her leave the dining room first as well as enter it first.

The head will probably be informed when all have finished and by rising will give the signal for all to leave. This is to be taken as the cue for everyone else to rise, replace his or her chair quietly, and exit in an orderly fashion. If you are at liberty to choose your seat in the dining room, don't make the head of the dining room feel as if he had measles by ignoring his table regularly. Sit there reasonably often anyway. If for any reason you must enter the dining room late or leave it early, go to the head of the dining room and ask to be excused.

GRACE

Most college dining rooms have grace preceding some meal of the day. You will soon learn the custom in this matter, but it is well to have it in mind so that you will not interrupt it by conversation.

In many college dining rooms, faculty members, seniors, or upperclass diners act as hosts or hostesses for the individual tables. You may, however, find yourself in a dining room devoid of experienced hosts or hostesses and therefore called upon to assume such duties yourself. As the head of the table, either host or hostess, you have two equally important and often simultaneous responsibilities: first, to make sure that the physical needs of each member of your table are cared for; and, second, to assume the social direction of your table by performing the necessary introductions, setting the standard of conduct and table manners, and initiating and guiding the conversation.

The details of taking care of the food wants of your table members will vary, of course, with the type of service provided in the particular dining room. In general, it is your responsibility to see that everyone is served before you begin to eat. Your beginning will be taken as a signal by the others to begin to eat too. You are also expected to time your eating so that you continue to eat as long as anyone else at the table is eating. If second servings are in order—as they usually are—then you should see that the serving dishes are passed or that the waiter re-serves each individual according to his wishes. If a wrong beverage has been brought by the waiter, or if a table member lacks any necessary article such as a fork or a napkin, he will appeal to you. You, in turn, will ask the waiter for whatever service is required.

Assuming the social direction of your table and setting the standard of conduct and table manners is important because the conduct of one table in a large dining room often affects the morale of the whole dining room.

INTRODUCTIONS

Your first social responsibility is to make sure that everyone knows who everyone else is. Ordinary introductions usually suffice; but when no one knows very many people at the beginning of a school year, it is particularly important that you and your table companions should concentrate on learning the names of all persons present. It will make you feel more comfortable and at home if you can call some people by name very soon. The following simple device for having everyone learn the names of all persons at the table may be used effectively.

1. Person on your right gives his or her name.
2. Next person gives first person's name plus his own.
3. Third person gives names of first person and second person plus his own—and so on around the table.

Of course it is only fair to reverse the order after you have made the complete circuit of the table to give Person Number One a chance to show that he has meanwhile learned all the names too.

Be as certain as you can of simple table manners, so that you can set a good example with ease. If you are uncertain of any point of procedure, don't hesitate to ask a staff member for advice. Your interest in doing the thing properly will be respected.

DIRECTING THE CONVERSATION

The principal technique at your command for deterring obstreperous members from flipping water with their teaspoons or engaging in equally adolescent pastimes is to launch such an interesting conversational drive that they will want to participate. A great deal of objectionable cutting up at the table comes from sheer boredom and the failure to recognize that it is really fun to find out what other people think. Almost any college student would rather talk about himself—what he has done, is going to do, believes in, or thinks about current campus problems and world politics—than anything else, if you give him the proper conversational lead.

The problem of keeping all voices down to a conversational level will probably be up to you, too. Setting a good example and using your sense of humor will be your most valuable techniques in maneuvering both the general conduct and the conversation to the level where you can be proud of them and of your managerial ability. And don't be lazy about keeping yourself supplied with conversational material. There are always the daily newspapers and the current magazines.

When you are a member of a table, you have almost as many

responsibilities as if you were the head of it. First of all, show due deference to the head of the table whether he or she is an older person or one of your own contemporaries. Don't be in a hurry to sit down yourself, but see that the head is seated first if you are near by. If food is to be passed at the table, start the dishes that are nearest to you, and see that they are passed to the head of the table first. As a table member you have the responsibility of gauging the speed of your eating to conform to that of the other members.

The essentially social aspect of dining as compared to mere eating is vividly emphasized by Admiral Byrd in *Alone*. He tells of how he found himself eating from a tin can, using his fingers, and eating while standing up when he was isolated from other human beings. Undoubtedly, it is the stimulus of dining with others that makes you try to observe the amenities and calls your real social resources into action. If the head of the table tosses the conversation ball, the symbol of sociability, to you, don't let it plop in the middle of the table. There's no use in his throwing the ball if all the catchers are mentally asleep. As for your general conduct, no college official ever expects more than that you should act your age.

Guests in the College Dining Room

College dining rooms in which only men or only women are regular diners create different problems for the seating and general treatment of guests than can be met by the usual rules of procedure, because there are not both a host and a hostess at each table. There are no set rules to cover the guest situation, but some arrangement should be agreed upon before the problem is imminent.

From a resident of a woman's hall comes this question:

> *"If I am entertaining my chemistry professor (a man) for dinner, do I precede him into the dining room or follow him, and which seat should I tell him to take?"*

Since he is a stranger in a strange land, you probably should ask him to follow you to your table. Assign him the chair at the right of the hostess as guest of honor. If you are table hostess, he will be on your right. If you are not the head of the table, you would take the seat on his right. The same arrangement would also be suitable if your guest were a woman, except that you would be free to take her arm and guide her through the door ahead of you toward your table. If a man were entertaining a man guest, he would follow much the same procedure; but if he were entertaining a woman guest, he would offer her his right arm and escort her to the position at the right of the head of his table.

YOUR PARTNER AS GUEST

If there are two guests who are more or less the guests of the whole table, one would be placed at the right of the head of the table and one at the right of the "foot" of the table. If you are entertaining more than one guest personally, you may place them wherever you like, so that they may see as much of the dining room as possible and have pleasant neighbors to talk with.

"When a girl invites a boy to an affair in the dormitory where refreshments are served, should the girl serve the boy or the boy serve the girl?"

The procedure here depends very much on the type of service and the amount of food being served. If it is only a matter of going to a window or station and picking up a plate of ice cream, it would seem that the girl, since she is the hostess, might serve both the boy and herself. The boy would do the same if the girl were a guest in his dormitory. If, however, a buffet supper is being served where half the fun is to see the beautiful table and help yourself to delicacies of your own choosing, then by all means both should go to the table and help themselves.

The boy would allow the girl to help herself first. If there were a salad or something particularly difficult to serve which required the use of both hands, then the host or hostess of the partners would serve both plates while the other one held them.

SECOND HELPINGS

Second helpings seem to be more of a problem in college dining rooms than in most other dining places.

Such questions as the following appear frequently:

"Is it correct to speak to a hostess about having the waiter pass something a second time?"

"Should one ask for a second helping or wait for the host to start a dish a second time?"

"Is it proper to take another helping of food if you still have some left on your plate?"

As was mentioned under the duties of the host or hostess, the caring for the food wants of his table members is one of the main responsibilities of the head of the table. If you are the head, try to have things passed before anyone has been in need of them too long. Whether you should ask for a second helping of something or wait until it is passed depends largely on whether or not you have timed your eating speed to that of the others at the table. If you have kept fairly well with the others, and they are also ready to have a dish passed, and the head still doesn't pass it, then you might with propriety ask if you might please have the dish passed. Normally the head will see that it is passed in good time.

It would seem quite all right to help yourself even though you still had some of that particular food on your plate, if you knew that you would thus avoid unnecessary passing, and if there were plenty in the serving dish.

Chapter Four

DINING IN HOTELS
AND RESTAURANTS

WHAT DO YOU DO IF *you don't know whether your escort can afford an entire dinner? Should he make suggestions from the menu? someone whom you know stops for a moment at your table? Do you introduce him to the others in your party? the check has been added incorrectly? Is a man considered a "tightwad" if he calls the waiter's attention to the error?*

WHO *orders the food? Does the man order for both, or does the woman give her order directly to the waiter? begins eating first—the man or the woman? seats the woman—her escort or the waiter?*

DO YOU KNOW *what table d'hôte and an à la carte mean on a menu? what an entrée is? demitasse? what* smörgåsbord *is and in what kind of restaurant it is found? the difference between chop suey and chow mein? what* spumone *is?*

THE SAME FUNDAMENTAL TECHNIQUES for the table hold for dining in hotels and restaurants as for dining at home, at school, or at the home of a friend. If you know how to handle your silverware and deal with specific foods, you should have little difficulty with the dinner itself. There are, however, a few items about checking wraps, finding a table, and ordering from the menu that are worth remembering.

Because of the high cost of luncheons and dinners in good restaurants, it is well to check on costs before you take guests. Many restaurants post the day's menu with prices in the window. Be sure to allow yourself some leeway for "hidden

77

costs" or at least be on the alert for them so that you won't be surprised if they appear in the final reckoning.

In a fashionable restaurant, the man checks his hat and coat in the checkroom before entering the dining room. The woman may check her wrap at the check room, in the dressing room, or she may wear it to the table and slip it back over her chair. The couple wait near the door until the head waiter gives them the signal to follow him to a table. It is often advisable to reserve a table in advance by telephone. If there are people waiting to be seated, the man should give his name to the head waiter so that he can be notified in turn when a table is available. The man permits the woman to precede him to the table. The waiter draws back the chair for the woman and seats her. He will see that she is given the more desirable seat, usually the one facing the door, or facing the center if there is a floor show. The woman may take her choice as to the side of the chair from which she will take her seat. A woman keeps her gloves and bag in her lap, not on the table. When one woman is entertaining another at luncheon or dinner she permits her guest to precede her to the table.

Two types of menu will probably be offered—table d'hôte and à la carte. Table d'hôte (literally the table of the host) means that the entire dinner is served for the price indicated. À la carte (according to the card) means that each item is priced separately and is to be ordered separately. Usually, ordering dinner à la carte is considerably more expensive than ordering from the table d'hôte menu. Sometimes different prices are listed following the entrées on the table d'hôte menu. That is, a dinner with a chicken à la king entrée will cost less than one with lobster or steak.

If the restaurant is new to you, and if you are particularly eager that the dinner be appetizing, it would be well to learn in advance what the specialties of the house are. Usually, good restaurants have two or three dishes for which they are famous.

There are a few French words that may be encountered on the menu whose meaning it is well to learn. *Potage,* consommé, and bisque all mean soup. *Potage* is the most general term. Consommé is a clear, thin broth; bisque or *potage* indicates a thick, rich soup. Croutons are small pieces of bread toasted or fried crisp and often served with the soup. *Plat du jour* means the "special" for the day. Hors d'oeuvres are appetizers served at the beginning of the dinner. Entrée is the main dinner course, consisting usually of meat, fish or fowl, and vegetables. *Fromage* is cheese. Demitasse (half a cup) means a small cup of black coffee.

ORDERING

The man takes the initiative in ordering the dinner and usually suggests items that he feels he can afford. The woman should have some consideration for the man's pocketbook. If he is a college student, the chances are that he is running on an allowance or is earning his own way through school. However, if the man is a family friend with a good income, there is no reason why she should not have the lobster à la Newburg if she wants it. The man should not order for the woman without first ascertaining her preferences.

The man gives the order to the waiter for his guest and for himself. In some restaurants, the customer is expected to write out the order for the waiter. As soon as the first course has been served to both, the woman is expected to begin eating.

If a woman is entertaining a man at her club or hotel, she may choose to place the order in advance. If the order is placed at the table she, as hostess, would give the order to the waiter and sign the check.

FOREIGN FOODS

A dinner in a restaurant serving foreign food is one of the real treats of metropolitan life. Often, however, one is very much confused as to how to order so that one may enjoy the best dishes that the house affords. Here are some of the most famous foreign dishes.

Soupe à l'oignon au fromage is soup with onion, toast, and grated cheese. The cheese is usually served separately so that the guest may use as much or as little as he likes. *Filet de sole Marguéry* is filet of sole baked with a specially prepared sauce. *Poulet* means chicken and is served *rôte au cresson* (roast with watercress); *grillé* (broiled), or *au crème* (with cream). Not to be missed as a dessert if you can afford them are the *crêpes Suzette*. These are pancakes but not the ordinary variety. They are carefully prepared and are then brought to your table and dipped into a very special sauce. Then they are rolled, sprinkled with sugar, drenched with brandy, ignited, and served.

German foods are, on the whole, simple but well prepared and flavored. You might try the *Sauerkraut mit Apfeln* (sauerkraut with apples), the *Leberkloesze* (liver balls), *Schnitzel* (pork or veal cutlets fried in butter and dressed with anchovies), *Hasenpfeffer* (ragout of rabbit), or *Sauerbraten* (beef stewed in brown sauce with vinegar added). The Germans are justly famous for their cookies, particularly their Christmas cookies (*Weinachtskuchen*). Try their *Lebkuchen* (life cake), *Springerli* (specially molded small cakes), *Pfeffernüsse* (pepper nuts), *Fruchtkuchen* (fruit cake), and *Kaffeekuchen* (coffee cake).

The main attraction for most Americans in Swedish restaurants is the justly famous *Smörgåsbord*. *Smörgåsbord* corresponds somewhat to the French hors d'oeuvres or to our appetizers, except that it is much richer in variety. *Smörgås* means bread; and *bord*, table, so literally *Smörgåsbord* means the bread table, although it is by no means restricted to bread.

The best part of a *Smörgåsbord* supper is that you take your own plate and go to the table, take as much as you like, and return as many times as you wish. You will probably find, in addition to a wide variety of breads and cheeses, anchovies, celery, olives, sliced cold meats, pickled herring, smoked salmon, grilled kidneys, mushroom omelet, eggs (deviled, baked, and creamed), scarlet shrimp, red and white cabbage coleslaw, and other delicacies prepared to the queen's taste.

Usually one does or one doesn't like Chinese food. There is no halfway business about it. The secret of Chinese cooking lies in the proper combination of foods and seasonings. Among the best known Chinese seasonings are Chinese sauce, or soy, used in place of salt; shrimp sauce; bean sauce; dried orange peel; dried onion sprouts; Chinese parsley; and oyster sauce. Chop suey, one of the most famous Chinese dishes, means fine mixture. M. Sing Au has described this popular food as follows, in *The Chinese Cook Book:* "It is a combination salad, done in a hot greased skillet to extract all the rare flavor of vegetables and made more alluring by the addition of Chinese condiments." You may have chicken, pork, beef, lamb, ham, or shrimp chop suey, as you prefer. Another famous Chinese dish is noodles—*mein* in Chinese. Chow mein means fried noodles. Here, again, you may have chicken or pork chow mein in various combinations. Chow sub gum mein is fried noodles with pork and vegetables. The *Foo Yung* combinations have eggs and vegetables for basic ingredients and are similar to our omelets. They may be had in such varieties as chicken, shrimp, green pepper, or watercress.

Well known and liked by frequenters of Russian restaurants is borsch, a vegetable soup made of beets, cabbage, and other vegetables and usually served with sour cream. *Shchi* is a cabbage and vegetable soup served with sour cream. Beef *Stroganov* is filet of beef cut fine, fried with onions, and served with a sour-cream base. *Blini* are pancakes served with sour cream and caviar or smoked salmon.

Macaroni, spaghetti, vermicelli, and ravioli (filled noodles) are four favorite Italian dishes. They are highly flavored with garlic, anchovies, mushrooms, olive oil, and peppers. Grated Parmesan cheese is usually sprinkled over them. The national soup of Italy is *minestrone*, a thick vegetable soup containing navy beans, rice or barley, and cabbage, well seasoned. Italian hors d'oeuvres are called *antipasto*. For dessert, *dolce ravioli* (sweet pastries) and *spumone*, which is somewhat similar to our ice cream, are specialties.

Most Mexican foods are very highly seasoned with chili or pepper sauce. Tamales (crushed corn mixed with minced meat, seasoned, and often wrapped in cornhusks and steamed), *tortillas* (cakes—usually corn), frijoles (Mexican beans), and *pozale* (pork and hominy) are favorite foods with Americans. The dish known to Americans as chili, or chili beans, a highly seasoned combination of kidney beans and bits of meat, is a universal favorite.

INTRODUCTIONS AT TABLE

Introductions are not usually made at the table unless the visitor stops more than momentarily or is invited to sit down. It is more friendly to introduce a person, however, if he stays for more than a few seconds than to let the situation get out of hand through delay. If a woman stops, the man, of course, rises and remains standing until she moves on or is seated unless he is pinned behind a table with too little space to stand. If this is the situation, he satisfies the convention by a half-standing gesture rather than embarrassing the woman with more commotion. Because of this convention, a woman should not tarry at a table. She should either nod and pass on or be seated. A man makes the same gesture to another man, but isn't quite so uncomfortable about sinking back into his seat as he is if a woman still remains standing.

PAYING THE CHECK

At the close of the dinner, the waiter will present the dinner check to the man. It is usually turned face down on a small tray. The man is not being penurious in the least to look over the items on the check and to verify the total. After he has looked over the check, he places a bill on the tray. When the waiter returns with the change, the man is expected to leave a tip of approximately 15 per cent of the bill for service. (See Tipping, pages 186 to 189.)

The waiter will help the woman with her wrap, if she has worn it to the table. The woman precedes the man from the dining room. The man leaves a tip of not less than fifteen cents for his hat and coat, and the woman leaves a similar tip with the maid in the dressing room, if she is supplied with towel, hand lotion, etc.

PARTIES OF MORE THAN TWO

If two women are enjoying a meal with one man, the man sits between them unless there is a built-in seat along the wall. In this arrangement the women are seated there and the man is seated on a chair opposite them. If two men are dining with one woman, the woman sits between the men except again if there is a divan along the wall where she is seated and the man she knows less well is seated beside her. The other man sits opposite her. Ordering in both instances will be done by the man who has invited the others to lunch or dinner.

When two men and two women are dining together, the women sit facing one another and the men sit to the left of their partners. If a group of four are using a wall table, the two women are given the divan seats and their escorts sit opposite them. For a group party the dinner is usually ordered in advance and may be paid for in advance, so that no check is presented to the host or hostess at the table. Seating arrangements will be cared for by the host.

Chapter Five

IN PUBLIC PLACES

WHAT DO YOU DO IF   *the girl you are with stops to talk with some-one whom you don't know?   you don't own a car, and the girl you are taking out offers to use her family's car? If you take the car, who should drive?   you are a Protestant and are accompanying a Catholic friend to church? Do you remain seated or try to follow the service?   you are a visitor to a church not of your own faith, and communion is served?   your escort suggests going to a play that you have already seen? Should you tell him that you have seen it or say nothing about it?*

WHO   *speaks first on the street, the man or the woman?   gets off the bus first, the man or the woman?   should contribute to the church offering—only the boy or both the boy and the girl?   hands the theater tickets to the doorman if the girl is giving the party?*

DOES   *a man walk between two women or nearest the curb?   a student lift his hat to a professor?   a man wear his hat in a hotel or a department store?   a man pay a girl's streetcar or bus fare if they have met accidentally?   a woman still have to remove her hat in the theater or movie?*

As soon as a person steps out of his own room, his behavior and dress become a matter of observation to others. Particularly does this hold true when he is in any public place. One general maxim which is always applicable with regard to one's appearance in public is: Don't be conspicuous. This generalization holds for clothes, make-up, conversation, and conduct. A well-bred person does not call attention to himself in any way when he is in any public place. He is careful not to accord to himself special privileges such as claiming the attention of a salesperson when someone else has been waiting longer or stepping ahead of others in a cafeteria line. A person's genuine courtesy and consideration for others are nowhere more noticeable than in public places.

ON THE STREET

Well-bred people
1. do not eat or chew gum
2. do not shout
3. do not congregate or walk in crowds upon the public sidewalks
4. do not indulge in any display of affection or in any other way make themselves conspicuous.

In particular, well-bred women do not smoke or replenish make-up on the street.

Custom is much less rigid now than it was a few years ago as far as appropriate clothing for the street is concerned. Women wear hats and gloves only if they choose to, and a woman who can manage gracefully without a handbag is free to do so. The weather more than anything else dictates appropriate clothing for the street as long as one stays within the bounds of relatively inconspicuous apparel. Many women even though not wearing a hat for summer shopping or sightseeing in the city do wear washable gloves to complete their costume. College women wear hats and gloves only for such particularly formal or serious occasions as a Sunday afternoon faculty tea, church service, or a funeral. They, too, frequently wear gloves even though they are not wearing a hat.

Clothing requirements for young men are correspondingly less rigid, but a man is still expected to fit into the setting or situation in which he finds himself. The college senior who normally cultivates the casual effect on campus turns up at his college placement office for an interview with a prospective employer in a conservative business suit, shirt, and tie.

Within recent years, a hat has become optional equipment for a young man in almost any situation. When he is dressed for the street, he wears a business suit, topcoat, and gloves if the weather requires them, and a hat if he chooses.

Traffic on the sidewalk as well as in the street moves to the right. If this general rule is observed, much of the staring into the other person's eyes with that unspoken question, "Which way are you going?" may be avoided.

A man usually walks nearest the curb when he is with a girl, stepping behind her to maintain this position when they cross the street. If he is with two girls, he still walks nearest the curb, on the theory that he is protecting them from oncoming traffic. The signs of the times indicate that this convention is weakening and that a man may, if he greatly prefers, walk between two girls. He neither holds the girl's arm nor offers her his when walking along the street. He does assist her over any particularly rough places and through traffic.

A man lifts his hat when he speaks to a woman acquaintance or performs some courtesy for her. He may lift his hat to an older man to whom he wishes to show respect; a student may properly do so to a professor.

When he is walking with a woman, a man must lift his hat to anyone to whom the woman speaks. This MUST is important. A man may not ignore the person to whom his companion speaks, even though he may never have seen the individual before. The same rule holds if he is walking with another man— he lifts his hat if his companion does.

GREETINGS

If there is a question of recognition, it is the prerogative of the woman to speak first to a man whom she meets. Naturally, when the man and woman know each other well, no such formality is practiced. Should a conversation ensue, the man asks permission to join the woman and walks along with her rather than detaining her on the street. A man walking with a woman will offer to carry any packages she may have; he will open any doors or make any inquiries for information that may be necessary. He will also take the initiative in ringing the doorbell, giving the apartment number to the elevator boy, and in inquiring for the person on whom they are calling. A woman, in turn, should not fail to acknowledge courteously any service rendered her by a sincere "Thank you."

A man in company with a woman asks her permission before smoking on the street. Although women smoke in many public places, the more fastidious ones do not smoke on the street.

Gum chewing is still bad form on the street as in any other public place. The improper disposal of gum has tried the temper of many a person unfortunate enough to have stepped on it. Make sure you are not responsible for causing such irritation. The removal of gum from streets, sidewalks, and public buildings costs the city of New York hundreds of thousands of dollars annually. A well-known mayor's suggestion that the manufacturers of chewing gum print on the wrapping paper a request that the paper be saved for the disposal of the gum seems a sensible one.

In Automobiles

Safety must, obviously, be the prime consideration in motoring manners. Any convention that involves a hazard of any kind has no justification.

In entering an automobile, the man allows the woman to precede him. If the man is driving and the car is parked where there is heavy traffic, he would ask her to excuse him and enter the car first rather than take a chance on entering from the left. When entering the back seat, the smoothest procedure is for the woman to sit at the left so that the man may follow her and be ready to open the door when the car stops. The man steps out of the car first and assists the woman to alight from the right side of the car. If he is driving, he would normally get out of the car and go around and open the door for the woman. If he has parked in traffic, the woman should open her door and step out first so that the man may follow her. If there are two women in the rear seat, the man alights from the car first and assists them.

THE BORROWED CAR

"Is it correct for a girl to use her own (or her family's) car if she is going out with a fellow who doesn't have a car? If so, who should pay the necessary expenses?"

"Should the girl let the fellow drive the car when it belongs to her?"

If the privilege is not abused, it is perfectly within the bounds of propriety for a boy and a girl to use the car belonging to the girl's parents if they have the parents' permission. The man should call for the girl at her home and stand the expense of the evening, including the gasoline used. If the girl requests the young man to drive, he may do so if he is sure of his skill in handling the car and if his driving license is in order and he is sure that the car carries public liability insurance as well as insurance on the occupants of the car and the car itself. Most young men who do not own cars are not in a position to pay for heavy damages to a borrowed car or for injuries to occupants. No young man should feel miffed if the girl chooses to drive her own car or that of her family.

Motoring manners, like all other kinds, are only matters of consideration for other people. Americans are widely accused of leaving their manners behind them when they start the motor of a powerful car. For the sake of safety as well as courtesy, you as a motorist should

1. keep your temper

2. obey all signals and road signs
3. use the horn sparingly and as a warning signal only. Do not use it so that you confuse the driver ahead of you, particularly if he is an elderly person or an obviously inexperienced driver
4. keep your eyes on the road and your hands on the wheel. One-arm drivers are out of date
5. signal to oncoming traffic your anticipated turns or stops
6. dim your lights for an approaching motorist, even though he is blinding you with his "distance" lights
7. avoid crowding the driver ahead of you
8. avoid passing on hills or curves
9. avoid taking more than your share of the road
10. make allowances in advance for the other driver's possible errors in judgment
11. be as courteous as you would be if both you and the other driver were on foot.

In Public Places

When entering an elevator, a man steps aside to allow a woman to enter first. If he is accompanying the woman, he gives the operator the number of the floor that they wish to reach. When women are present, a man removes his hat in the elevator of a hotel, apartment house, or club. He may do so in a department store or office building elevator, but convention does not demand it. He need not remove it while walking through or shopping in a department store or when walking through a hotel lobby. He would, however, remove his hat if he were talking with a woman in a hotel lobby.

A man permits a woman to enter the door first—even if it be a revolving door. If possible, he opens the door and holds it for her. A woman should always acknowledge this courtesy with a "Thank you."

If a woman is meeting a man in a hotel lobby, she permits him to seek her out if she arrives first. If he arrives first, as is said to happen occasionally, he watches for her and does not permit her to stand or sit alone.

Shopping often puts a severe strain on the manners of both the customer and the salesperson. The truly gracious and well-bred person will pride himself upon his courteous and considerate treatment of anyone who serves him in any capacity, even though the other person may be discourteous. The admonition of one mother to her young son is worth repeating: "Remember, son, you are courteous to others because you are well-bred, not necessarily because they are."

ON BUSES AND SUBWAYS

A man permits the woman whom he is escorting to enter a bus ahead of him. If there is a long line, he cannot be expected to wait until all women have entered, but he does permit the woman who is accompanying him to precede him. The same is true of subway travel. If each subway passenger would extend even the simple courtesy of taking his own turn instead of jostling for a better place, the bad American subway manners would be considerably bettered. Even though someone else is rude and inconsiderate, try to keep your temper. Others around you will bless you and you will feel better yourself.

Even in this day of casual manners, a man offers his seat in a public conveyance to an older woman or to a woman who has young children with her. The same courtesies are expected from a young woman. The woman to whom the seat is offered should accept it and express her appreciation for the gesture.

When alighting from a bus, if it is convenient the man alights first and assists the woman.

If a man and a woman meet accidentally, it is not at all necessary that the man pay for the woman's transportation. Most women would prefer, under such circumstances, to pay their own way and do not expect any gesture toward this end on the part of the man.

IN CHURCH OR SYNAGOGUE

Since the purpose of the religious service is the worship of God, the only fitting attitude is one of reverence. Conversation preceding or during the service is out of order.

Women are expected to wear hats and gloves. In many places of worship it is considered a mark of disrespect for a woman to enter with her head uncovered. For example, at the entrance to the small chapel at Stoke Poges, near which Gray wrote his *Elegy Written in a Country Churchyard*, there is a notice that women may not be admitted without having their heads covered. In orthodox Jewish synagogues, men, too, are expected to wear hats.

The matter of where to sit is usually solved for you by the usher, who knows whether or not certain pews are reserved for members of the church. In most churches now, all seats are free, but some communicants who have sat in the same pew for years are particular about having their own places. It is always proper to ask an usher to seat you in the section of the church that you prefer or in a friend's pew, if you have obtained his permission.

"When a Protestant accompanies a Catholic friend to church, should he remain seated during the entire service, or should he stand when his friend stands and remain seated when he kneels?"

Most of us feel comfortable in the church that we are accustomed to attending, but we feel out of place and ill at ease in services in which the ritual is different from our own. The air of formality makes us particularly conscious of our behavior. It is well to inquire of one's friend in advance concerning the question of what to do at certain points in the ritual. A visitor can give no offense in either a Catholic or an Episcopal Church if he sits during the entire service. If, however, he wishes to follow the service, he is at liberty to do so. In no case does he criticize if the service happens to be different from that to which he is accustomed. The general rules of procedure are that the congregation stands for praise, sits for instruction, and kneels for prayer.

"Should one take communion in a church other than his own?"

Some faiths have "open communion," which means that anyone who wishes to do so may partake of the bread and the wine. Others have "closed communion," which means that only their own members may partake. Usually the clergyman will make it clear that visitors either are or are not invited to participate. If you are uncertain regarding the practice of the church in which you are a visitor, it would be better not to participate in the communion service.

"What should a girl do if her boy friend offers to pay her offering in church?"

There are no "paid admissions"; the offering one makes is entirely voluntary. If one is able to do so, he will make an offering, however small. If he is not able to contribute, he is free to enjoy the service just the same.

If a young man accompanies a girl to her place of worship, the girl will no doubt want to make her own contribution. He, too, will probably contribute something. If the young woman accompanies him to his church, she may be less likely to contribute but may with perfect propriety do so.

IN THE THEATER

"If your escort suggests going to a play which you have seen, should you tell him you have seen it or go to it?"

It is usually necessary to make arrangements for a theater engagement some time in advance, since tickets are often difficult to obtain. If there are a number of plays from which to choose, the young man may suggest several to the girl and let her make her choice. If the girl has seen one of the plays that is suggested, she should not hesitate to say so. The man wishes to give her pleasure and does not want to spend money to have her bored.

It is tactful for the girl to suggest to the man that it is not at all essential to her enjoyment of the evening that they sit on the main floor, which is usually called the orchestra. She may even take pride in the fact that she is still able to climb to the second balcony. The man will, of course, take care of the arrangements regarding tickets as soon as the choice of play has been made. It is less expensive to buy tickets directly from the box office, as it is customary for ticket agencies to make an additional service charge on each ticket they handle.

If there are to be any special arrangements for dress, they should be made at the time the invitation is extended; otherwise it is assumed that street clothes for the woman and business suit for the man are entirely acceptable. First nights often see the patrons in formal evening wear but not the ordinary theatergoer.

It is important to arrive on time so that you will be in your seats before the curtain rises. The man gives the tickets to the doorman and steps aside to permit the girl to enter the theater first. He then looks about for an usher. He shows his stubs to the usher, who will lead the way to the seats. The girl precedes the man. If no usher is readily available, the man will take the lead in finding the seats. In either case, he permits the girl to enter the row first, and he always sits nearest the aisle.

When two couples are together, each man holds his own tickets and presents them, unless one of the men is host for the party. If a girl is affluent enough to give a theater party, she gives the tickets to one of the men before they reach the theater. When several couples in the same party are finding their seats, each man follows his partner in walking down the aisle and in entering the row of seats.

If others in the row have already been seated, you should say, "I'm sorry" or "Excuse me, please." If you stumbled over the person's feet or knocked her handbag from her lap or in some other way inconvenienced her, you would say, "I beg your pardon." The men who are seated should rise to permit you to pass them more easily. Women may exercise their judgment in the matter. If there is room for those entering to pass, women may remain seated and simply turn so that there is as much room as possible. Passing others in a theater row is awkward, at best. You will, of course, use your intelligence in getting into your seats with as little inconvenience to others as possible. Most people believe that the best procedure is to face the stage as you edge your way into your seat.

A woman removes her hat before the curtain rises if there is any likelihood at all that the hat will inconvenience the persons seated behind her. If the woman in front of you fails to remove her hat, it is not discourteous to say, "I'm sorry, but I can't see. Would you mind removing your hat?" It does, however, require courage.

A man usually removes his hat and overcoat in the lobby and checks them at the check room. The woman may also check her wrap there. If, however, she wears it to her seat, the man assists her in removing it after she is seated and throws it back over the seat.

While the curtain is up, conversation is out of order. Needless to say, any display of affection is also.

It is entirely permissible to leave one's seat between acts for a drink of water or a cigarette or a breath of air. The man lets the girl precede him in leaving the row and in walking up the aisle. Anyone leaving his seat during an intermission should return to it before the curtain rises. A man should not leave a girl alone between acts unless he asks her to excuse him.

It is discourteous both to the players and to those sitting near you to leave the theater just before the final curtain. The business of putting on wraps and reaching the aisle is disturbing and annoying. After the play is over, the man assists the girl with her wraps and rescues his own. The girl precedes him from the row and out of the theater.

IN THE MOVIES

The general atmosphere of the movies is much more informal than that of the theater, and the conventions are accordingly less precise. Tickets are readily obtainable at the door in most movie theaters, and there is usually no trouble about getting seats.

If a man and a girl are attending a movie together, the man will purchase the tickets at the window. The girl may step inside the lobby to wait for him to join her, or she may stand alongside him in the line to chat with him if she prefers.

If there is an usher, the girl precedes the man down the aisle and into the row of seats. The man, as in the theater, sits nearer the aisle. The girl removes her hat immediately if there is any chance it might prove distracting to those seated in back of her.

Conversation, comments on the picture, and demonstrations of affection are in equally poor taste at the movies as in the theater. If you will remember that you, along with every other individual in the theater, hold one ticket and are entitled to the space of one seat and no more, the question of disturbing others will not arise.

It is not considered discourteous to leave during a picture. When leaving, you should say, "Excuse me, please," to those whom you inconvenience.

AT CONCERTS AND LECTURES

There is only one important rule to be observed in attending any concert. You are expected to maintain absolute quiet during the performance of the different numbers. The weight of social disapproval will descend upon you quickly if you rustle a program, talk, or in any other way disturb those about you. Edna St. Vincent Millay's poem "The Concert" expresses beautifully the feeling that many people have when they attend a concert. One person who chews gum audibly or who talks during the performance may ruin the evening for a number of people around him.

Performers before an audience are entitled to appreciation of their efforts, which is usually registered by applause. At a symphony concert, applause is expected at the close of an entire number. The audience usually remains silent between the parts, or movements, of a single rendition, but you can tell whether applause will be acceptable by watching the conductor. Don't be the one to break the mood of the music inadvertently by bursting out with untimely applause. Applause is out of order at any religious service.

A lecturer who is asked to face an audience with newspapers and books ready to be opened the minute the lecture becomes slightly boring begins under a difficult handicap. Any speaker who has ever tried to keep his attention on his address in the face of having even one person very obviously reading a newspaper knows that the ninety-nine who want to hear him suffer because of the inconsiderateness of the one who is bored. It hardly seems unreasonable to ask that a person who dislikes lectures remain away or that, if he is required to attend he do so graciously. On campus this holds for your college professors as well as for the occasional visiting lecturer.

AT ATHLETIC CONTESTS

Courtesy is an integral part of the sportsmanship of the playing field. Almost everyone would grant that it should also be a characteristic part of the behavior of the spectators but that too frequently it is not. "Check your manners here—you will not use them in the stands"—might be the sign outside many an entrance gate, judging from the booing and uncomplimentary remarks that are heard within! Loud and bitter criticism of officials, opponents, and even of one's own team often bespeaks ignorance of the fine points of the game. Especially, however, does it indicate lack of putting one's self in the place of the person criticized. One explanation of this sort of bad behavior is that people often permit themselves to do or say things when they are surrounded by many other people behaving badly, that, as individuals, they would not like to claim credit for. Perhaps it would be a good rule to follow that one should never permit himself or herself to behave as a part of a group of students in a way that he would not be proud to behave as an individual.

Booing an official is a personal discourtesy of which no one would be guilty if he had ever tried to officiate at any contest himself. After all, both teams have shared in the selection of officials who are, as a rule, persons of integrity. It is only fair to give them credit for doing their best to make fair decisions and to be philosophical enough to realize that the "breaks" will probably even up by the end of the game.

Even at mass spectacles, such as football and basketball games, certain courtesies are observed. Everyone takes part in the "welcome yell" to both teams. Men remove their hats, and everyone rises when the Alma Mater of either school is sung. Partisans of both sides applaud an injured player as soon as he gets to his feet, whether he continues to play in the game or not.

Spectators at a golf or tennis match are much more restrained in their expressions of approval or disapproval than spectators at football, baseball, or basketball games. At a tennis match, no one applauds while the ball is in play. One waits until the end of the rally. The applause is usually confined to hand clapping, although sometimes an enthusiast will call out "Well played!" or "Beautiful shot!" Applause is reserved for a particularly good play rather than for an error on the part of your favorite's opponent. If you have occasion to move about at all, you should wait until the players are exchanging courts, as moving objects in the stands may be distracting to them.

During a golf shot by anyone, friend or foe, informal game or match play, everyone remains silent and motionless. Be sure to stand far enough away from the person swinging the club so that he will have no possible fear of hitting you. The boys with the ropes and the size of the gallery will determine largely where you stand in relation to the player during a big match; but in an informal match, you should stand far enough away from the player so that he is not worried about touching you with his club or hitting you with the ball, but where he can see where you are and will not be uneasy about you. You should take care not to step on his line of putt or stand on it beyond the hole or throw any shadow on it. You don't want him to think that you are the cause of his failure to "hole out."

Chapter Six

DATES

IF YOU   *were calling a girl for a date, would you ask, "What are you doing tonight?"   were busy on the evening suggested for a date, would you suggest another specific time to the young man when you would be free?   joined two girls of your acquaintance while they were having Cokes, would you feel obligated to pay for them?   wanted to arrange a date for a friend who was visiting you, would you call a boy whom you know but with whom you have never had a date?   had taken a girl dancing, would you consult her before trading dances?*

WOULD YOU   *expect to go into the house with a girl after a date unless you were invited?   know what to order for refreshments when you didn't know how much the boy could afford?   ask a boy to your house dance even though he had never asked you for a date?   ask a boy to a second coed bid function without his having entertained you betweentimes?   think a Dutch treat was out of order if you knew the boy well?   date another girl if the girl to whom you were pinned was too far away for you to see her often?*

MOST SOCIAL SKILLS are directed toward pleasing other people in general, but the social skills of dating are usually directed toward pleasing one other person especially well, and anyone knows how important, yet how difficult, that can be.

Dating covers an unbelievably large area of social relationships, some of whose practices have remained the same for many years, but also some of whose practices are in such rapid process of change that only the best informed of the younger generation themselves can be expected to know what is being done. In this area, probably more than in any other area of social relationships, young people want to know what is acceptable to their contemporaries—if one may judge from the sort of questions that they ask. They are not particularly concerned about the law laid down by any authority whose claim to this role is based on observation instead of participation. This is understandable: after all, most of the younger generation are intent on dating—and pleasing—each other.

In order to answer some of the hundreds of detailed questions about dating with some semblance of authority valid in the eyes of the younger generation, the help of some of their own acknowledged leaders was sought. Delegates to a recent national convention of the senior women's honorary organization Mortar Board, and men students of their choosing, were selected as a sampling of acknowledged leaders who might reasonably be expected to know what was being done by their contemporaries. These persons were most generous in their efforts to interpret the current mores of their campuses in those areas of social relationships between young men and women which are changing rapidly. Discussion based on their interpretation of current acceptable practice on their campuses is indicated in the following discussion by "Mortar Board questionnaire." Treatment of the subject based on informal discussion with many students and observable practice in a college situation is indicated by "Student discussion."

It goes almost without saying that one cannot discuss current problems of this sort without using the language of persons whose problems they are. As far as a large part of the current younger generation is concerned date is a far broader term than social engagement. It may be a noun of double meaning or a verb of great importance. A date may be anything from a few minutes spent over a Coke to the most formal of college junior proms with dinner before and breakfast afterward. Or the term may refer to the man or girl whom one is dating as well as to the occasion.

Dates—both the persons and the affairs—may be of considerable variety. There are, for instance, just ordinary dates, when the boy and the girl know each other more or less well and the boy takes the initiative for issuing the invitation to the girl for some form of evening's entertainment. Then there are those inventions of the socially minded for getting young people acquainted with each other referred to popularly as blind dates. That doesn't mean at all that either the boy or the girl can't see, but rather that he or she has not been seen by, "the party of the first part." Then there are coed bids, or occasions for which the girl takes the initiative; and Dutch treats, for which either the boy or the girl may take the initiative but for which each assumes his own financial obligations.

Judging from the quantity and variety of student questions about general dating procedure, there seems to be an infinite number of details of the subject which one needs to have at his fingertips. How well must I know a girl before I may ask for a date? How shall I ask for a date? How shall I accept or refuse? How shall I call for a girl? How shall I act when the boy calls for me? What is there to do besides dancing and movies? Do I have to have a car? How much money is it necessary to spend? Whose responsibility is it to suggest going home? How do I say "Thank you" properly? How? How? How? Much, however, as one needs specific information, he needs more to remember the general rules of courtesy and thoughtfulness. It is difficult to be displeasing company if one concentrates on making the other person comfortable and at ease. And this simple rule holds for either the boy or the girl.

Date Procedure

The question of whom one may have a date with is, of course, largely a matter of personal choice. Far less formality enters into the matter than it did in the days of our grandparents. It is still considered necessary, however, for young people to be introduced by friends; or to meet each other at a properly conducted social affair sponsored by a responsible group; or to become gradually acquainted in the classroom, laboratory, student-activity workshop, or business situation before they may have social engagements together. A thoughtful girl will still wish to avoid the criticism of accepting the invitation of a man whom she has not met through accepted channels, and a boy will be reluctant to put either the girl or himself in a position to be criticized on this score.

Getting acquainted with members of the opposite sex is certainly the first step in dating, and student leaders in assaying current practice judge that it is acceptable to be friendly to all and to make an effort to get acquainted with people you don't know.

On all campuses sampled, from Maine to Texas and from Oregon to Florida, the answer was "yes" to both of these questions:

"Should boys and girls speak on campus if they have not been properly introduced but have seen each other at different times?"

"Are blind dates socially acceptable?"

Often a distinction is made between those blind dates which are arranged by friends and those which are arranged more or less impersonally through campus date bureaus. Needless to say, the percentage of satisfactory dates is apt to be higher when someone knows both the boy and the girl and feels that they would be congenial. On the other hand, everyone wants and needs to know lots of other young people on the campus without standing on too much ceremony. Date bureaus sponsored by reliable organizations which try to match up students for dances or parties and all-college mixers held in gymnasiums or union buildings may be very real aids in starting the social ball rolling. Any boy or girl will make the best of the situation if he doesn't happen to be assigned someone especially congenial, but he will also, undoubtedly, be equally skillful at terminating the date if there is any real reason to do so.

Girls wonder:

"Why do boys call up and ask, 'What are you doing tonight?' instead of asking for a definite date, which you may either accept or refuse?"

This question makes fairly clear what every girl hopes for in an invitation—the freedom to choose whether or not she will accept it. And if a boy will think the matter through, he will see that it is much more of a compliment to him for the girl to accept if she has the chance to refuse him than if he gives her no choice.

If you wish to extend an invitation to do a specific thing, then say so definitely; for example: "Hamlet is at the movies. Everyone says it is very good. Would you like to see it?" Or "Johnnie Jones's band from Michigan is playing for the mixer a week from Saturday. Would you like to go with me?" Don't hesitate to give the girl an occasional opportunity to suggest what she would like most to do. You will get considerable insight into her tastes. Always pay her the subtle compliment of implying that she is a busy and popular person but that you hope she will have the time and inclination to accept your invitation.

The acceptance formula is, of course, "Thank you, I'd like to go." Difficulty arises for the girl when she already has an engagement for the particular time suggested yet does not wish to discourage the young man. Her best reply in that case is probably a genuine "I'm sorry, but I've already made plans for Saturday evening. Another time, perhaps, I'd love to go." It is probably better for her to leave the suggestion of another specific time up to the boy rather than suggesting it herself. (Student discussion.)

If a girl has accepted your invitation, then by all means do her the honor of calling for her inside of her residence and returning her to that place, unless she specifically requests you to do otherwise. Aside from consideration of the neighbors, it is no compliment to any girl to sit in your car and honk the horn for her or to whistle for her to come outside to meet you. Be prepared to greet her family if she lives at home or her housemother or housemates if she is living away from home. And remember that there is nothing she wants quite so much as to be proud of the way you look and act in the presence of these people who know her so well.

ARRIVAL AND INTRODUCTIONS

If you are the girl, the boy will probably be especially grateful to you if you are ready to greet him when he arrives, particularly if he hasn't met your family or your housemates and would have to spend the time with them until you are ready. You should, by all means, do the young man the honor—and your family, or whoever else happens to be around, the courtesy— of introducing him to them. You are the hostess and should take the initiative in this.

To the question:

"Is it ever proper for a man and girl to meet at some designated place to go on a date rather than at the girl's home or residence?"

Most student leaders answered "yes" but qualified the answer by specifying that it was "okay" to meet on campus or at the library for an informal date. For an evening occasion the circumstances would be rare, indeed, when the boy would not call at the girl's residence for her.

"Should a girl respond to affection when she has no desire to do so?"

"How can you avoid 'parking,' good-night kisses, etc., without hurting the boy's feelings?"

These are questions that undoubtedly deserve serious answers from anyone who aims to be practical. The only advice that seems practical for such situations is "Keep the light touch." The following paragraph from the chapter headed Petting—or the Pursuit of Happiness, from the booklet *How to Get Your Man and Hold Him*, expresses this philosophy very well: "Without making too much of a point of it, avoid settings that might prove too tempting from a petting point of view. If *he* suggests parking the car on a deserted country lane or sitting on an isolated strip of beach to watch the moon go down, don't demand to be taken home immediately or threaten to get out and walk if your request is not granted. Your best weapon is flippancy. Tell him (laughingly, of course) that he is much too dangerous for you to be alone with him in any such romantic atmosphere. Instead of being annoyed, he will doubtlessly be flattered that you consider him a temptation." Such handling of the situation seems feasible if your own emotions are not involved to any appreciable extent.

A somewhat different problem is presented by the girl who is genuinely fond of a boy when she asks,

"Is it permissible to 'park' with a boy if there is no other place to be alone?"

There is no use dodging the issue; no one can be around a college community without observing a considerable number of "parkers." The plea is made to any official who remonstrates about the parking in front of sorority houses and dormitories, "Well, you would rather have us park here than out on the highway, wouldn't you?" It seems that you must determine what you consider good taste in the matter and deny yourselves or indulge yourselves accordingly. The other boys and girls around you are subject to the same emotions and the same lack of privacy as you are. If you really have a keen sense of your social obligation to be a constructive factor in the formulating of the social mores of your group, you will consider well before you grant yourself any parking or petting privileges that you would be unwilling to grant to the rest of your group in the same time and place. In other words, don't be guilty of making an exception in favor of yourself. It's not cricket.

And only for emphasis, something that you girls already know is repeated by quoting one of the "Normal Young Man's" admonitions to any girl who aspires to be the "Model Girl about Town," from Margaret Fishback's *Safe Conduct:* "Don't delude yourself that we men never kiss and tell on the girls who kiss promiscuously. We mean to be gentlemen, but in our cups at the club [or at the fraternity house—this insertion is added], we are shameless gossips about the girls we know are shameless neckers."

Suitable entertainment for a date covers a wide range of activities in these times when young men and women do almost everything together. It is true that dancing and movies probably constitute a very great percentage of dating entertainment, but they are not by any manner of means the only things to do. Almost any girl will tell you that it is not the amount of money spent on a date that determines whether or not she has a good time. (Student discussion.)

The determining factors are much more likely to be a congenial group of other girls and men to help make and share the fun and the genuine interest of both the particular man and girl in seeing that the other one enjoys himself. Picnics, hikes, roller skating, ice skating, tennis, swimming, bridge, or whatever the favorite indoor game of the moment may be are certainly highly satisfactory alternates to dancing and movies, part of the time at least. Even a walk to the library or to the corner drugstore for a Coke is a favorite dating activity if you would like a chance to exchange a few ideas and explore each other's mental resources.

EXPENSES

"What do you do when your date asks what you would like to do, and you have no idea how much money he has to spend or what he likes to do?"

Your safest course is probably to suggest several different things for entertainment representing a variety of price and interest range, any one of which, you can insist, would make you happy. At least this gives the boy a chance to "inkle" his inclinations even if he does turn the decision back to you. (Student discussion.)

The question of transportation was back of this question that was asked many times:

"Is it proper to use the girl's car for a date if the man has none? If so, who should drive?"

Student leaders, both men and women, were almost unanimous that it was acceptable to use the girl's car or her family's car and equally unanimous that the man would be expected to do the driving. This, indeed, puts a special responsibility on the man. He should be doubly certain of his ability as well as doubly certain that the car insurance and his driver's license are in good order. There are, however, apparently a few women who feel that they should drive their own cars and any young man should accept that feeling understandingly if his girl happens to feel that way.

One always wants to time the asking for a date strategically so as to get a "yes" answer. That probably accounts for the frequency with which this question appears:

"How far in advance should a boy ask a girl for a date?"

It may be that the answers of women student leaders to this have more significance than have the men's answers. In any case almost all of the women say that the request for a date for a formal party should come over two weeks in advance, while fewer than half of the men allow that much time. For an informal party, however, the men's and women's replies are similar. The majority seem to feel that a week in advance is about right. For an individual date there is a sizable vote for one week in advance, but the majority of both boys and girls seem to think two, three, or four days is sufficient.

Again in their answers to this question:

"Is it proper for a girl to accept a date if a man asks her just a few hours in advance?"

the men and women differ somewhat. The great majority of girls say: "Yes, if . . ." and specify that how well the couple know each other should be the determining factor usually. There seems to be a feeling that it is all right to accept if you think that there is some reasonable explanation possible as to why the man hasn't issued the invitation sooner—the implication being that they think it would be better if the invitation were earlier. The men on the other hand say "yes" or "yes, if the girl wants to go," without any further implications one way or the other.

No girl expects to be transported by car or taxi everywhere she goes. Unless she is in formal clothes or the weather is bad, she is as capable of walking or riding on the bus as a man.

The pattern of conduct that you work out during your first date or so with a given person is obviously of the greatest importance, because it determines not only the success of the moment but probably whether or not there will be future dates. Besides, the fairly simple matters of acceptable techniques for asking for or accepting a date, introductions to family or housemates, and so on, which are more or less the same for everyone, every individual has to make up his own mind and determine his own personal standards regarding petting and drinking. To those of you who are having difficulty making up your minds on these points, it should be a comfort to know that hundreds of other girls and young men are struggling with the same problems. In other words, you do not have to decide any certain way in order not to be different from your contemporaries. They don't know the answers either, and your judgment, in all likelihood, is as good as theirs. So don't be afraid to use your own head and make your own decisions in line with your own ethical standards.

Boys by the hundreds are wondering whether or not girls expect boys to kiss them good night on the first date. Girls by the hundreds are wondering whether or not boys expect the privilege of kissing girls good night. The boys kiss the girls because they think that the girls expect it; the girls let the boys kiss them because they think that the boys expect it! It would seem feasible, on the one hand, for the girl to reflect on whether or not she personally wished to grant any privileges to a young man of slight acquaintance who, perhaps, was seeking privileges only because he thought that she might expect it of him.

On the other hand, the boy might reflect whether or not it was any personal compliment to him to have a girl who knew him only slightly grant him privileges only because she thought that he expected them, and not because she liked him especially. Intelligent, honest discussion of these problems by groups of girls and boys who enjoy each other's respect and confidence should help them to understand the conflicting points of view somewhat better.

PETTING

Demonstrations of affection between you and the boy or girl you are dating are the most personal of matters and should certainly be based on genuine personal affection. No person, girl or boy, should let his ever present fear of being different force him into expressions of affection that he doesn't mean. Good taste requires now, as it has required for years and years, that you keep any show of affection a private and personal matter by not permitting yourself any privileges in the presence of other people. Most people, although entirely capable of expressing affection for special persons themselves, find it exceedingly embarrassing to be subjected to the public demonstrations of others.

The intolerance of chaperons for the activities of certain young couples is more often based on what they consider the bad taste of public demonstration of affection than it is on the disapproval of the affection itself. Nor is it only the elders who are embarrassed by this sort of thing. The question comes from both boys and girls, "What should you do when the couple you are double dating with starts necking to the point where it is embarrassing?" What *can* you do?

To the question:

"Is it expected that you will kiss your date good-night on the first date?"

the women students answer with an unequivocal "no" and only a very few of the college men say "yes."

On the other hand, to the question:

"Is it proper to kiss your boy friend good-night publicly on the front steps or in the entrance lobby or should you do it in private?"

the majority of men and women students alike say "yes" with the addition "of course, it would be better in private, but where is there any privacy?" There are numerous qualifying notes emphasizing casualness to the effect that "a good-night kiss is all right, but not a long drawn out affair."

Many girls who are probably well trained in the art of prompt-

ness for all ordinary occasions wonder whether they should keep
their "dates" waiting for the sake of the effect. In reply to the
question:

> *"Is it good taste to keep one's date waiting for a few minutes
> after he calls?"*

the only reasonable reply is that it is inconsiderate to keep
anyone waiting when it isn't necessary. It ought to be possible
to achieve a good effect in a more constructive way. Besides,
some men get irritated if they have to wait around needlessly.

DRINKING

The problem of drinking is so bound up traditionally with
morals as well as manners that it is difficult to consider the matter realistically without offending some whom one would not
wish to offend. Any adult, however, who has worked closely
with many young people in recent years may be forgiven if he
or she more or less unconsciously associates the two words
"problem" and "drinking" together. The tremendous growth
of Alcoholics Anonymous testifies that drinking and problem
are synonymous in all too many instances. While there are an
infinite number of aspects to the problem that deserve discussion and attention, one, at least, is of particular concern to
young people in the present discussion and should be pointed
out immediately.

The state laws in many instances are very strict against drinking or possession of liquor by anyone under the age of twenty-
one. Failure to observe these laws can and often does cause
embarrassment to young people. Quite aside from any discussion of drinking, advice to know the law and observe it seems
superfluous, but it's still good advice. As to a discussion of
drinking itself, it is no good saying that "nice" boys and girls
never drink; too many who qualify as desirable citizens sometimes do drink. Perhaps it wouldn't be an overstatement, how-

ever, to say that these boys and girls qualify as "nice" not because they sometimes drink but in spite of it. One thing seems certain from observation and discussion with young men and women: no one *has* to drink a highball or a beer or a cocktail to keep from being a "wet blanket." You can always order a Coke or root beer to see you through. (Student discussion.) The fact is generally recognized that some people *do* prefer them to stronger drinks, and most people will concede you as much right to your taste as they have to theirs. Don't be afraid to act according to your own convictions. In all probability, they will stand the test of time as well as the next person's. People don't particularly mind your refusing to join their drinking, if you don't moralize smugly as you do it. (Student discussion.)

It goes without saying that no lady or gentleman "gets drunk." At least, anyone who does so usually ceases very shortly to belong to either of these categories. To achieve the heights of a true "gentleman and a scholar" is hard enough without trying to do it sans part of your wits. It is almost unforgivable lack of consideration for either a boy or a girl to put his or her partner of the evening in the position of having to assume responsibility for a drunken date. If you are the sensible one of the two people and can see where your partner is heading, try to deter the weak-willed one before it is too late. Cut the evening short with an improvised appendix if you must, but don't let yourself in for more trouble than you have to.

If you are the boy in the case and the girl is the one who hasn't maintained her discretion, take her away from the party and keep her from making a spectacle of herself if you possibly can. It is hard enough for a boy to live down making a fool of himself, but a girl's reputation is even harder to regain. If you are the girl who finds herself with a drunken escort on her hands, you will have to manage well if you are not to remain in a very conspicuous position. If the boy has any masculine friends about, don't worry about him. They will see that he gets home. (Student discussion.)

If there are no other men to depend upon, the situation is more difficult. No one will blame you if you simply leave him to manage for himself as best he can. (Student discussion.)

If the boy is someone you care especially about in spite of his inconsiderateness, you might call a taxi, pay the driver fairly generously, and ask him to take the offender home. You may not like to have to fend for yourself, but you can always call a taxi and be on your own way. Even if you haven't been prudent enough to take your "mad money" with you, the taxi driver will always wait for you to go into your house to get his fare.

DRIVING AND DRINKING

One further point was mentioned by several young people in discussion: Under no circumstances let the boy (or girl) drive a car if he (or she) has been drinking. In the first place, obviously, an accident is more likely than usual to occur; and in the second, if one does occur, no one will have any sympathy for a driver who has been drinking. He is wrong, as far as the public is concerned, no matter what the facts of the case really are.

The above discussion assumes that you may be caught in a relatively normal social situation where you have to handle the matter of drinking if it arises incidentally in the course of the evening. The only thing you can do, man or woman, is to handle the situation as expertly and as inconspicuously as you can.

To let yourself become involved in a deliberately planned "beer bust" or "beer blast," as students sometimes call beer-drinking picnics or parties, is something quite different again. If you, either as the man or the woman, know that the picnic that such and such a crowd from so and so's house is planning for Saturday evening will turn out to be a "beer bust," then your cue is to speak up in favor of some other entertainment for the evening or a different picnic with a different crowd for you and your date. There's no use walking into trouble with the university authorities, or, in many instances, with the state law, with your eyes open. And there will be many other people who will be more than glad to join you for a picnic with Coke and coffee to wash down the hot dogs. Don't be one of those uninformed students who say innocently when it is too late "I didn't know there was any rule against it"; or, worse still in the eyes of college deans, one of those who excuse themselves by saying "everyone else does it." Good sense demands that you know the rules and act accordingly. Integrity and honesty demand that you accept responsibility for your own actions.

Men and women are unanimous in their reply to:

"If a girl has no wish to drink, should she do so on a date if only to be sociable?"

and the reply is "no."

Obviously both men and women are expected by the majority of the students answering the questions:

"Should a boy drink if his date doesn't drink?"
"Should a girl take a drink if her date doesn't drink?"

to make up their own minds about drinking and not be influenced by their dates. There are more women and men, however, who feel that it is unacceptable for a girl to drink if her date doesn't, than feel it is unacceptable for a boy to drink when the girl does not. In other words it looks as if there is more chance for the boy to keep two people from drinking— himself and his date—than for the girl to exercise a corresponding influence. This, it should be pointed out, is contrary to the age-old dictum that the girl sets the pattern of social behavior. The present generation seems to vest the man with responsibility in this case.

The same general attitude that it is acceptable for both men and women to follow their own inclination pertains to smoking also. Almost all of the men and women replying say "yes, if she wants to" in reply to:

"Is it proper for a girl to smoke if her date doesn't smoke?"

Incidentally, a great majority of both men and women believe that it is current practice for women to supply their own cigarettes on a date if they smoke.

In all ordinary situations, the girl has the responsibility for suggesting the time for starting home. And if you are the boy involved, you must expect her to do this and realize that she is suggesting going home because she feels that she should and not because she is bored. Your cue is to accede to her suggestion gracefully even when you are having a wonderful time. Your status with her family will certainly be better if you get her home at a reasonable hour; and, if she is subject to a definite schedule for door-closing time, it is imperative to get her to her place of residence promptly, unless you want her to suffer disapproval for your negligence.

Upon arrival at her home, it is the girl's privilege to invite the young man to come in for a few minutes if both the time of night and the inner status of the house warrant her issuing the invitation. As the boy, you shouldn't, however, assume that the privilege is yours unless it is extended to you. If you are living away from home and chaperonage in the house is provided until a definite hour, then, of course, you will be guided by the time and by your own inclination.

THANK YOU

As for expressing your appreciation for the evening's fun— don't hesitate to do it. Any young man has the human urge to please and to want to be approved of. Warm friendly appreciation of what others try to do to please you is never out of order.

It is up to the boy to thank the girl for the evening.

Every time a girl must refuse a date for any reason, and she would really like to go with the boy, she is faced with the problem:

"What is the best way to refuse a date so the man will ask you again sometime?"

The answers of the men leaders on campus are what she really needs to know. Dozens of them run in this vein:

"Explain why you can't go—thank him—and ask him to call again."

"Be forthright."

"Be sincere."

"Be friendly."

"Tell him you'd really like a rain check."

The problem is a little different if a girl doesn't want ever to go out with the boy:

"What is the best way to refuse a date so that you won't hurt the man's feelings, but so that he will know you don't want to go with him?"

To this question most of the men plainly say there is no way to do it, but the man who writes this reply at least has a suggestion:

"There is no way to keep from deflating the male ego, but probably the better way would be to refuse him the date every time he calls until he grows tired of calling—this way he thinks he has dropped the girl and not she him."

Breaking dates is always difficult at best, but almost all voters agree that it is permissible if one has a legitimate excuse, such as illness or the arrival of one's family. The warning is issued, however, that the excuse given must not be that you find that you are going to be "busy" or that you have to study. Be specific, and this holds for girls and boys both, whichever one is breaking the date. (Mortar Board questionnaire.)

"How do you tactfully suggest going to a rest room when you are on a date?"

This matter often presents a problem to both the boy and the girl, for either one may wish to be excused and yet not know how to present the matter tactfully to the other one. If you remember that probably your partner will appreciate a few minutes' respite as well as you would, it may make it easier for you to suggest it. If you are the girl who wishes to be excused, you may certainly say to the boy, "I'd like to stop in the dressing room a few minutes. May I have my compact and bag? Shall I meet you here in a few minutes?" If you are the boy who wishes to be excused, you might say to the girl, "You would probably like to stop in the women's lounge a few minutes. Let me take you there and then I'll be back and pick you up in about five minutes." If you wish to be a very thoughtful and considerate man, you will do something of this sort sometime during the evening whether you wish to be excused yourself or not.

Perhaps you have had dinner and are going on to an entertainment. It shows considerable thoughtfulness and poise on your part if you are forehanded enough to ascertain the location of the women's lounge and, after you have finished dinner and are putting on your wraps, can say, "You probably think you have to powder your nose before we go on to the movies. The women's lounge is through this archway and to your left. I'll see you back here when you are ready to go."

If you are the driver of a car on a trip of any distance, take occasion to stop at modern well-equipped service stations every so often. Get out of the car yourself, and indicate to your passengers that they are free to get out and stretch if they like—that the "bus" is stopping for a few minutes.

Dances

Dances constitute a large and important area of dates, judging from the hundreds of questions relating to them asked by members of the younger generation. Of course, the techniques which apply to dates in general apply also to dances.

Just as for any other date, a girl needs to be invited to a dance far enough ahead of time for her to make her plans accordingly. Campus leaders seem to agree that two to three weeks before the function is about the proper time to issue the invitation for most formal dances. If the dance were the most important one of the year, the time might be somewhat longer; for an informal or more usual affair, the time might be from ten days to two weeks. (Mortar Board questionnaire.)

Any girl will appreciate her escort's telephoning her two or three days before the dance to make final arrangements as to the time when he will call for her and to inform her of any details that he has planned such as a dinner before the dance or the names of the couple with whom he has arranged to double date.

Should it be impossible for either the man or the girl to keep the engagement made for a dance, it would be a courtesy to offer to find, with the disappointed partner's permission, a substitute, so that the other person would not have to miss a function for which all arrangements had been made.

DRESS

When the invitation is issued—usually a personal one, whatever the nature of the function—information should also be given as to whether the dance is formal or informal so that the girl will know what kind of dress is expected of her. Girls almost always check with their feminine acquaintances if there is any question as to type of dress in order for any particular informal party.

Specific suggestions for the choice of clothes, for nail polish, gloves, and other accessories for both men and women, are given in the chapter entitled Personal Appearance. In general, one would conform in dress to the nature of the dance, formal or informal.

Campuses vary in their customs regarding sending corsages for dances. If you do not know the local custom, you will have to check with some of the other men who are attending the same dance to see what is being done. If you find that the others are sending flowers, you should manage somehow to do it too, for a girl who doesn't receive flowers when everyone around her is exclaiming over theirs is apt to feel neglected.

Further details of corsage selection and the wearing of flowers are given in the chapter entitled Extending and Receiving Courtesies.

"Should a girl expect to be taken to formal and other affairs, on a nice night, in a car?"

"Does a girl object to walking rather than using a taxi going to and from a dance?"

Cars and taxicabs are always a convenient mode of transportation but not always a necessity. The girl's costume, the distance, and the weather should probably determine whether you may walk or ought to provide transportation. No sensible or appreciative girl minds walking a short distance or riding on a bus on a fine evening in a short dress. On the other hand, formal clothes and evening slippers are expensive items of a girl's wardrobe. You probably wouldn't ask her to walk more than a few blocks even on a fine night if she were wearing her best party clothes and certainly not out into any weather that would ruin them. (Student discussion.)

If one drives to a dance, it is courteous to offer to deliver the young woman at the door, say, "I will meet you at the dressing room shortly," and then park the car and return to the building. She may not mind going along with you, but you can find out by offering her the chance to go inside at once.

RESPONSIBILITIES UPON ARRIVAL

Seeing that the girl's wraps are properly disposed of and that she has an opportunity to rearrange her hair and make-up in the women's dressing room before making her public appearance for the evening are your first duties upon arrival at the dance. The responsibilities from then on are largely determined by the variety of dance attended. Probably the most usual sort is the so-called program dance during which some of the dances of the evening are exchanged with other couples of your immediate group. The sentiment is strong among both women and men campus leaders that the girl should be consulted before any trade is arranged. (Mortar Board questionnaire.) The trading of dances, of course, for a strictly program affair should be arranged whenever you can do it most advantageously—probably before you come to the dance. If the situation is more informal and the program is not set, trades can be made during the evening as the occasion arises. In any event, it is the man's responsibility to find the girl's new dancing partner; to see that she is never left stranded between dances; and to return to her own escort of the evening any temporary dancing companion with whom he may have danced.

At some dances, no numbers are exchanged with other couples: a straight program is danced. This practice simplifies the man's problem in keeping his program straight, but it doesn't make for a particularly sociable evening. At other dances, which are not program affairs, there may be a number of unattached men, popularly known as "stags." When there are extra men present, the matter of cutting in causes problems.

CUTTING IN

Cutting in is considered acceptable dance technique on a
majority of campuses for certain sorts of functions like "mixers"
or other all-college affairs. The sentiment is definitely against
permitting the practice at dances where it is not in general
use, such as at a program dance. On the other hand, if it is a
cut affair, generally accepted practice dictates that the girl
must dance with whoever cuts in, even though she is enjoying
her current partner. (Mortar Board questionnaire.)

If you want to remain popular with the couple you are cutting
in on, you will not cut back on a man who has just taken a
girl from you; you will allow any couple to dance around the
room at least once before you cut in; and you will not cut in on
partners who are sitting out a dance.

The question of who is the more uncomfortable of two
people who get stuck with each other is a weighty one, for
each feels the responsibility of making himself or herself more
agreeable or entertaining than he or she is at the moment, and
the bewilderment of wondering what to do overtakes all sensible
reaction to the situation. The girl, after two or three dances,
may ask her partner to take her to the dressing room or to her
escort (if he is not dancing) or to her friends. Turning the situation off as a joke is recommended if you can bring yourself to it!

The technique for asking for an individual dance follows
the same principles as asking for a date. No girl likes to be
asked bluntly, "Have you this dance taken?" Maybe she hasn't
and is feeling self-conscious about it and isn't sure you will ask
her if she says "No." You might make it easier for her by saying
simply, "May I have this dance?" That still gives her a chance
to refuse you if she must.

"May a girl suggest not finishing a dance?"

It is the girl's privilege to suggest sitting out a dance or to stop during a dance if she wishes. The man never suggests stopping until his partner or the music stops, except in unusual circumstances. Similarly, the woman suggests returning to the floor when she is rested.

Judging from responses of student leaders to the following questions, reciprocity in the exchange of dance invitations is not necessarily expected. Obligation is not acknowledged, but the returning of an invitation is looked upon as a nice gesture.

> *"If a girl has entertained a man at her dorm or sorority dance, is he obligated to entertain her in return?*
>
> *"Is a girl obligated to pay a boy back for dates by inviting him to her dorm or sorority functions?"*

Coed Bids

Coed bids cover that area of dating in which the girls take the initiative and try to reciprocate some of the social favors that the boys have showered upon them. The amount of financial responsibility and initiative that the girls carry varies with the different varieties of coed bids. On many campuses, one day or one evening a year is set aside as "Sadie Hawkins' Day" or "Gold Diggers' Night" when the ordinary course of events is reversed. On these occasions, the girls issue the invitations to whatever the big social affair is; they send the corsages (often of vegetables or gumdrops); furnish the transportation; pay for the refreshments; carry the boy's make-up kit; and see him safely home—all in a spirit of mock seriousness.

Coed bid affairs that occur much more frequently than those mentioned above are dances, dinners, or open-house functions sponsored by groups of women students for which the girls themselves are the hostesses. In this category are residence hall, sorority, or other organized house dances which are open only to the women of the organization and their invited guests. Also included are those dances sponsored by various all-campus women's organizations for the purpose of promoting sociability and raising money.

For Sadie Hawkins' Days every campus will have its own rules, and every girl will try to outdo every other one in the entertainment of her date. On the other hand, the more usual coed bid function of a house dance carries certain fairly definite responsibilities and obligations for the man who is invited and accepts the hospitality and courtesy extended to him. The girl has paid him a distinct compliment by inviting him, and he is expected to perform as gallantly as he knows how.

WHOM ONE MAY INVITE

There seem to be some specific practices in the area of coed bids that enjoy fairly wide acceptance, if one may judge by the agreement in the conception of "generally accepted practice" expressed by almost all of the Mortar Board representatives and the men leaders expressing opinions. They agree that a girl may invite a man whom she has known in classes, or to whom she has been otherwise introduced, to a coed-bid function on the campus or to her own house dance, even though he has never asked her for a date. On the other hand, the vote is almost as strong that it is improper to invite a man to two parties without his having reciprocated betweentimes. The opinion also is that a college girl who invites an outsider to a non coed-bid function on the campus is expected to pay for the bid; that any girl inviting any man to almost any social function should extend the invitation from one to two weeks ahead of time. (Mortar Board questionnaire.)

It is almost a unanimous opinion of the leaders that generally accepted practice on their campuses includes the privilege of asking a boy whom one has never dated oneself to have a date with a visitor; the expectation is that the boy will arrange for transportation and pay for any intermission or post-party refreshments of an ordinary coed-bid function, such as a residence hall or a sorority dance. (Mortar Board questionnaire.)

Apparently men think they should reply promptly to an invitation from a girl, for their answer to:

> *"If a girl has invited a man to her dorm or sorority dance and he has not replied within a week, is she free to invite somebody else?"*

is a strong "yes," although a few think it would be nice if the girl checked first.

While group coed-bid affairs are very popular and are an accepted part of the social pattern, the regular individual date pattern is still for the boy to issue the invitation. Less than a seventh of either men or women answer "yes" to this question:

> *"Is it all right for a girl to ask a fellow to go on a date even if it isn't a girl-invite-boy affair?"*

Obviously girls should still be very sure of their ground before taking the initiative in this matter.

Girls are expected to take the initiative, however, by most student leaders in the instance referred to below on the theory that they are hostesses and are therefore responsible for making the party go well.

> *"During an open house or trade party, when the girls are in their own residence, is it proper for them to take the initiative in asking the boys to dance?"*

The appropriateness of girls' telephoning boys also comes in for some discussion. To the question:

> *"Is it proper for a coed to phone a man   to invite him to a party?   to make last-minute arrangements?   to visit?"*

both men and women student leaders answer unanimously that it is proper for the girl to phone a man to invite him to a party or to make last-minute arrangements. They are also agreed that it is not acceptable for a girl to call a man just to visit. In fact there is considerable sentiment against prolonged unnecessary use of the phone when more than likely someone else needs to use it for business.

"If a girl has bought the ticket for a function, should she hand it in or give it to the man to hand in?"

"If the occasion does not necessarily require a corsage, should the girl tell the man not to send flowers?"

Boys and girls alike, apparently, think it appropriate for the man to hand in any tickets, regardless of who has paid for them. They consider it proper for the girl to tell the man not to send flowers if the occasion does not require them.

Dutch Treats and Who Pays for What

Dutch treats, in so far as they present a problem in social usage to the younger generation, apparently refer only to Dutch treats between boys and girls. The old-fashioned kind when a girl pays for her own way with a group of girls or a boy pays his own way with a group of boys does not seem to present any difficulties.

To the question:

"Is it ever proper for a boy to ask a girl to go Dutch? When?"

the replies from the men are about ten to one that it is proper *if* the couple know each other very well or if the occasion is an unusually expensive one such as a trip out of town to a concert or theater that a man could not afford. The great majority of girls agree with this opinion although the percentage is a little less than with the men.

"If you and your date are having a Dutch-treat dinner should each pay his own check or should the girl give the money to the man to pay both checks?"

Boys and girls are agreed almost unanimously that the girl should give her money to the man and not pay her own check.

It is practically the unanimous opinion of the leaders that on their campuses men do not pay for girls' lunches when they eat together, unless it has been a specifically arranged date. Nor is a boy expected to pay for all the Cokes just because he happens to join two girls who are in the midst of sipping theirs. Each one pays for his own. In fact there is currently a great deal of social intercourse of this sort among young people both on campus and in business that adds greatly to their opportunities to share their pleasures and increase their circle of friends.

Chapter Seven

SOCIAL COMMUNICATION

WHAT DO YOU DO IF *you have just met your dinner partner and can't think of anything to say? you are waiting for a girl, and another man who is dating another girl in the house sits down near you? Should you start a conversation? you have made an untactful remark? you receive a last-minute dinner invitation and know that you are a "fill-in"? you are invited to dinner and can't tell from the invitation whether dress is to be formal or informal? Should you call the hostess?*

WHAT CAN YOU TALK ABOUT *on a first date? during and after dinner when dining out with a man's parents? to a celebrity, if you don't know anything about his particular field? to a faculty member whom you do not know at all?*

DO YOU THINK THAT *a young woman should call a young man if she hasn't heard from him for several days? if a girl likes something about a man, she should compliment him? it is possible to correct another person's grammar without being impolite? colored stationery is good form for social correspondence? it is all right to type a personal letter? a boy should write to a girl without previously having asked her permission? printed cards of thanks are acceptable?*

TODAY, our conversation and correspondence are carried on by word of mouth, by letter, by telegraph, by radiogram, by telephone. In spite of the ease of communication, however, and of the fact that we "study English" from our earliest youth, communication through any one of the available channels is not easy for most of us. For one garrulous Mrs. Grundy who monopolizes the conversation and the telephone line, there are probably a dozen of us who are tongue-tied in the presence of a stranger, can think of nothing better than the weather to talk about on the first date, chew the ends of our pens in composing a thank-you note or condolence letter, and pray for the earth to swallow us if we find ourselves confronted with the necessity of talking to a celebrity.

Conversation

People who can carry their end of the conversation interestingly are in demand for dinners, parties, dates, and other social affairs of all kinds. For these reasons and others, we long to be good conversationalists. Unfortunately, there is no royal road to achieving this goal, no easy way to success in ten lessons.

There are, however, some basic essentials of conversing pleasantly with other people which we can strive to master—the ability to use the English language effectively; a background of information on a wide range of topics; a mental calmness which enables us to enter into the give-and-take of a social situation; a pleasing voice; and a genuine desire to contribute our bit to the group of which we are, for the moment, a part. Obviously, the wider our range of interests is, the easier it will be to fit into different social groups.

Carrying on a conversation may be compared to taking part in a game of catch. The ball is tossed to you; you receive it and toss it back, or you muff it and retrieve it yourself or expect the next person to do it for you. You may be playing in a two-cornered game, a three-cornered game, or a five-cornered game. Of course, in the two-cornered game you receive and toss more frequently than in the others. Your main objective is not that of the pitcher who is trying to get three strikes on the batter or that of the tennis player who is trying to jockey his opponent out of position so that he can score. It is rather to return the ball so that it can be caught, juggled, and passed on by the person to whom you are throwing it.

SOME RULES OF THE GAME

Conversation, like any other good game, has underlying principles that make the play stimulating. The following tactics will help you to play your position well:

1. Think before you speak. First, last, and always, *think before you speak.*

2. Be courteous in conversation. Interruptions, contradictions, tactless or unkind remarks will stamp you indelibly as a discourteous person.

3. Practice give-and-take in conversation, erring on the side of being absorbent to what is said rather than allergic to it.

4. Keep your mind on your conversation, neither letting it veer from lack of interest nor sending it out after topics that are not at home in polite company. Operations, personal affairs, and sometimes politics and religion are dangerous subjects of inquiry; too often you get an answer!

5. Speak personally of people only when you can say something pleasant and agreeable about them, and then confine your remarks to their activities and achievements rather than their personal characteristics.

6. Remember that once is enough when telling an incident and that enthusiastic repetition of details that were funny the first time will make them anything but that the second time.

Dr. Lillian Gilbreth, the noted woman engineer, tells a story that illustrates well the "receiving and tossing" aspect of the game of conversation. She says that some years ago she was at a tea when a young boy aged thirteen came in. He appeared extremely uncomfortable and ill at ease. Someone said to him, "Hello, Charles. How are you today?" Charles managed a "Fine" and reached for the sandwiches. Nothing more in the way of conversation could be extracted from him. Eight years later, Dr. Gilbreth again met this same young man at a tea.

He was then a senior in college. He came into the room, greeted his hostess and the guests standing near her. Someone again said to him, "How are you today, Charles?" "I'm fine, thank you," replied Charles, "and you?" Telling this story, Dr. Gilbreth remarks that somewhere in the eight years intervening between the two teas, the young man had learned to toss the conversational ball back with an "and you?" You will have mastered one of the most important elements of conversation when you learn to toss the ball back.

EQUIPMENT FOR CONVERSATION

Conversation in most circles turns sooner or later to current events; current books and magazine articles; current plays, musical events, and art exhibits. Busy though you may be, if you can manage to read a daily paper, even sketchily, or listen to at least one daily radio or television news broadcast you will have a fairly good idea of what is going on in the world. A weekly reading of *Time* or *Newsweek* or of the Sunday edition of *The New York Times* or *The New York Herald Tribune* will give you a background of information that will enable you to enter into a discussion of current events with some feeling of being informed. The book-review sections of *The New York Times* or *The New York Herald Tribune* will give you a conversational knowledge of the new books and a lead as to which ones you may care to read. You should also be familiar with some, at least, of the widely read magazines of general interest such as *Harper's Magazine, The Atlantic, Reader's Digest, Life, Look, The Saturday Evening Post, Coronet, The Saturday Review* and *The New Yorker*. It is an excellent idea to browse through the periodical room of your library and familiarize yourself with the magazines there. You are sure to discover one or two new ones which will be of interest to you.

YOUR VOICE

Is your voice pleasant to hear, modulated, resonant, distinctive? Is it too loud, shrill, rasping, whining? The quality of your voice either contributes to or detracts from the first impression that you make on everyone you meet; that impression *can* be a favorable one. If you are in doubt about your own voice and its appeal, it is a simple matter to have a voice record made at a reputable speech clinic and to analyze it for possible improvements.

Pitch, strength, tone quality, and expression are the major factors in one's voice. The rate of speaking is also a determinant of how pleasing one's voice is to others. A voice of low pitch is more pleasant to the ear than a high-pitched one, and a voice that has a variety of inflections is to be preferred to an uninteresting monotone. You can profit by observation of the distinctively deep and expressive voices that some radio and television speakers have developed. The strength and intensity of the voice should be carefully controlled so that one speaks neither too softly to be heard nor so loudly as to be irritating. Some of us have to watch this quality, particularly when we become excited. Expression is probably the most personal voice factor, and the interested, enthusiastic person will make his enthusiasm apparent in his speech.

Articulation, natural and distinct, is one of the primary requisites of the well-developed voice and is cultivated by practice and care. The timeworn illustration of the meticulous speech of radio and television announcers is just as good as it ever was; and if we all had the requisite time and a seashore, we could, like Demosthenes, speak through pebbles and above waves to enhance the clarity of our own speech. Few things are so exasperating to a listener as having to strain to decipher the rumble of slurred speech.

VOCABULARY

Vocabularies have a way of growing from contact with good writers and good speakers, but they also have a way of remaining static if not given attention. Perhaps we are not all sufficiently conscientious to emulate the young woman who stuck small cards in her dressing-table mirror as a device to remind herself daily of five new words (marked with pronunciation and meaning) that she wished to add to her vocabulary. However, making a new word one's own is a simple matter if practiced consistently. Practice it on your friends. Perhaps they will be interested in learning it too.

Adjuncts to speech that can be interesting or unpleasant are mannerisms. Among the common faults are affectation; the over-use of slang and profanity; repetition of "Well," "As I said," "You know what I mean," or other unnecessary phrases; and touching or patting or standing too close to people while talking with them. Dangling sentences carelessly cut off and never finished are another common irritant. The sensitive and considerate person will analyze any mannerisms that he has and eliminate those which may give offense.

A speech characteristic for which only good can be said is the habit of completing one's replies, saying "Yes, Dr. Harris," rather than simply "Yes."

A word about slang and profanity. Slang is a spicy addition to speech if it is used as any spice should be—sparingly. Over-use of slang has two undesirable results: It loses its brightening effect, and it stamps the user as careless. The admonition regarding profanity that is given to cadets at the United States Military Academy at West Point may well be heeded by young men and certainly by all young women:

"The idea that profane or obscene language bespeaks strength of character or manliness is a wholly mistaken one. . . . In ordinary conversation, even where only men are present, foul language is ill-bred and undignified." *

STARTING A CONVERSATION

There is no one best way to start a conversation with someone whom you have just met or whom you do not know well. About all that can be said is that such an occasion is no time to "fight it out on this line if it takes all summer." If one topic doesn't get a response, try another and another.

If you have just been introduced, the person performing the introduction can be of great help by suggesting that you are both interested in writing or bridge or golf or etching. If he knows of any common interest, he should mention it.

If you are having a first date with someone and aren't very well acquainted or are just talking casually with an acquaintance, there are always such perennials as the team, movies, tests, courses, professors, campus politics, the things the "house" is doing, campus speakers, and possibly a book or two that both have read. People and current events are the topics with the most general appeal. Even to this question:

"What can one talk about during and after dinner when dining out with a fellow's parents?"

the same answer holds: Talk of items of mutual interest, of people and places and current events. Because many people's political and religious views are strongly tinged with emotion, it is better to avoid them in the early stages of acquaintanceship. Personal questions are likewise taboo.

If you will keep reminding yourself that most people are more interested in their own lives and the things that touch them directly than in anything else, you will nearly always have a good conversational lead. Most people are interested, first of

* Elinor Ames, *The Correct Thing at West Point.*

all, in the things that *they* are doing, in *their* family, *their* possessions, *their* achievements. Secondarily they are interested in these same things about you. If you can find the other person's interest, you will not have much difficulty in keeping the conversation moving. Such an attitude can, of course, be carried to the extreme. One man has said that many of the people he has met try so hard to be charmingly interested in him that they are bores! He prefers that they lose themselves in some topic of interest to them and let him do the listening for a change.

Nevertheless, we are all familiar with the tales of persons (and you may even be fortunate enough to know some) who prove delightful companions not because of what they have to say but because of their faculty for listening. A real interest in another's remarks, thoughtful attention to what he is saying, and an intelligent question now and then will practically insure the success of a conversation, however one-sided. And it is well to remember that nothing makes one so welcome a companion as making the other person feel that his clever remark was just what your funny bone was waiting for.

Usually, if you are in the presence of a renowned person, you need not worry about the conversation. The famous person has probably been a guest at so many functions that he or she is adept at keeping the conversation going. If it lags, ask him a question about some aspect of his work. It is often a good idea to read a bit about the man or woman before you attend a reception in his or her honor, so that you will be able to ask intelligent questions.

At a home affair or in a mixed group or in the classroom, there is no priority about who is to start the conversation. To be friendly and interested in the other person is only courteous. On the street, the woman speaks first to the man.

"If another girl's date comes into the living room of the resi-

*dence hall and sits down to wait, should one speak and start
conversation? If so, which one speaks first?"*

The man in such a situation is the guest, and it is, therefore,
the responsibility of any girl who happens to be present to
put him at ease by talking to him. A man who is waiting for
his partner of the evening is at perfect liberty to introduce himself to another man who is also waiting, and to start a conversation.

*"At formal dinners, is it better to be very free and natural in
your speech and actions or to act more reserved and dignified?"*

You should always be natural and enjoy yourself without
being conspicuous. Of course, there can be no harm in dressing
up your manners as well as yourself in honor of a party, but
you should avoid the necessity for any improvement over your
everyday speech and actions. Dressed-up manners have a way
of betraying their user.

*"Could social problems be considered all right for formal con-
versation—e.g., sex, marriage, vice, and so on?"*

Such topics as these had best be reserved for more intimate
discussion where controversy can be stimulating and not dis-
tressing.

In casual street and campus meetings and in conversation, it
is the privilege of the girl to terminate the conversation. In a
telephone conversation, the one who initiated the conversation should close it. Of course, one would temper any closing
so that it would not be abrupt and so that the other person
could say a last word if he chose.

TELEPHONE CONVERSATION

With the rise of the telephone to its present place of importance in communication have come points of courtesy that

should be respected. Particularly in a large residence group the problem of length of telephone conversations sometimes approaches distracting proportions, and it is necessary for each resident to limit the length of his calls when others wish to use the telephone.

If the instrument is being thoughtlessly monopolized and it is necessary for you to make a call, you might courteously ask if you might telephone for a certain reason. The most effective treatment for consistent offenders is group disapproval.

In answering and speaking over the telephone, one's voice and manner are all-important. When answering the telephone in a home situation, one always says "Hello." The person calling would reply "Hello, this is Mary Johnston. May I speak with Mrs. Perry, please?" If Mrs. Perry has answered the phone, she will then reply "This is she" or if someone else has answered she will say "Just a moment, please, and I will call her." The important points to remember are (1) identify yourself and (2) make it clear whom you wish to speak to. It is not your concern who answers the phone, so you should not ask "Who is this?" nor should you put the other person in the position of asking you who you are. Man or woman, you use your given name in identifying yourself—never any title; this is John Jones speaking or this is Mary Fuller speaking, not Mr. Jones or Miss Fuller.

On a college campus, residence units usually have a set form for phone answering in their particular house. "Good morning. This is the Gamma Gamma Gamma House," with or without the addition of "This is Jerry Brown speaking." As soon as Jerry knows who is wanted, he will offer to call him to the phone or to take a message if he is not at home.

It is now considered acceptable for a girl to telephone a man if she has a valid reason for doing so. On the other hand she should not call just to visit about nothing in particular nor should she call so often or so regularly that the man's house-mates have reason to be critical of the interruptions she causes.

Calls during business hours should be held to a minimum, and one should never hold an extended social conversation over a business telephone. For the person in business to make long calls is to usurp time that does not belong to him. For an outsider to call a friend at business is a source of embarrassment to the business person, who probably is literally busy.

There are convenient times for receiving telephone calls, and there are inconvenient times. Consideration for the family or fellow residents of one's friend should make one think several times before telephoning at mealtime or beyond a reasonable hour at night—ten-thirty or eleven o'clock. It is a simple matter to ascertain the regulations about phone calls in large residence groups. If one will abide by these, he may save his friend embarrassment from a late or inconveniently timed call.

SPECIAL CASES

"Is it proper to eat while carrying on a conversation with another person who is doing most of the talking yet talking more or less to you?"

Give-and-take there must be in dinner-table conversation; but since there must also be eating, we can only strive to combine the two in pleasantly alternating intervals.

"If a girl likes something about a fellow, should she compliment him?"

"If someone should compliment you on your appearance, what should be the proper answer?"

Compliments, to both men and women, are welcome if they are sincere and subtle. Acknowledgment of a complimentary remark can be made graciously by "Thank you" or "I'm glad you like it."

"What should one say to people after they have had a death in the family?"

Upon the occasion of a death some expression of sympathy is always appreciated by the family, but the less elaborate the expression the better. A simple "I am sorry. Is there anything I can do?" is sincere and sufficient.

"Is there anything one can do to get out of a situation as when listening to a prejudiced person talking politics, religion, and so on, especially when the person is older or commands respect?"

If possible, one should find a loophole in a controversial discussion through which he can draw the conversation to less disturbing topics.

"How can one best pass over an embarrassing remark?"
"What should you do when you make an untactful remark before you realize it?"

Blundering or tactless remarks, embarrassing questions and comments, and malicious gossip are always difficult to deal with. The best procedure is to ignore the comments if possible and to steer the conversation into more pleasant channels at the first opportunity. If someone has been really offended, an apology should be made.

"Is it possible to correct someone's grammar without being impolite?"

No one likes being corrected in group conversation, and efforts at improvement of grammar and diction had better be reserved for members of the family or personal friends who may consider them as favors and not insults.

"Is it bad manners to be outspoken?"

Frankness and sincerity are never bad manners but tact must temper any frankness that may hurt another person if it is expressed. There is no virtue in outspokenness for its own sake.

"If two people are engaged in conversation and you have to speak to one of them, how do you excuse yourself?"

If you find it necessary to interrupt a conversation, wait for a break in the discussion if you can. Then go up and say to the person, "I beg your pardon, may I speak to you a moment?" Then stand aside, and wait until the person can excuse himself and come to you.

"What type of joke should be told in front of ladies?"

Clever jokes that won't be offensive to anyone and that won't mark you as crude are always acceptable. But be sure they're funny. Vulgar jokes or stories are embarrassing and in bad taste in any group, regardless of whether all men, all women, or some of both are present.

Correspondence

Social correspondence includes letters to your friends, bread-and-butter letters, thank-you letters, invitations and announcements, messages of congratulation and of sympathy, and notes of acceptance and of regret.

Letters are a substitute for you in person. They represent you when you cannot be present yourself; and, if you later become a celebrity, they may represent you to posterity. It is true that there are rules and regulations about the paper you should use, the color of your ink, and the form of the communication, but your friends and family who are eager to maintain contact with you and know what is happening to you will agree that the important thing to them is for you to write.

Most of us might not find our social correspondence such a

chore if we had a place for writing letters and had the necessary equipment at hand. If you expect to do your part to keep up your connections with your distant friends, have one place where stationery, pens, ink, blotter, and stamps are available.

STATIONERY

If you would be sure of correctness always, white notepaper of good quality should be your stationery choice. Good stationery is also supplied in various delicate shades and colorings and is in good taste for most social correspondence. Letters of condolence, however, should be written on white paper. Ruled paper is not used for social correspondence. The increasing popularity of the air-mail service has had an effect on the kind of stationery manufactured. Much of that now in use is purposely of light weight so that several sheets may be sent via air mail without exceeding the weight limit.

Most stationery used for social purposes is folded once so that there are four writing surfaces. Single sheets are entirely acceptable, however. It is not wise to use very small paper and envelopes, as they are more likely to be considered an affectation than a convenience, as well as to be lost in the mails.

When a folded sheet is used, the fold comes at the left of the first sheet. The one guide as to the order in which pages are to be used should be the ease with which the person who is to receive the letter can follow it. The most widely accepted usages are either to fill the pages in order as one reads the pages of a book or to use sheets one and four and then to open up the folder, turn it sideways, and use the full length of pages two and three. If only two pages are to be filled, pages one and three are usually used. Authorities disagree upon the sequence of pages, so your best guide is to remember that this is a detail of relatively little importance in comparison with the subject matter of your letter and its general appearance.

HEADINGS AND MONOGRAMS

Stationery carrying the name or the name and address of the writer is widely used. The form is

MARION HARPER

or

MARION HARPER
225 FERRY STREET
CHICAGO 26, ILLINOIS

A married woman usually has her stationery printed

MRS. WILLIAM F. HAYES
171 NORTHRIDGE DRIVE
NEW HAVEN 4, CONNECTICUT

A married woman who is a celebrity in her own right would, of course, use her maiden name if she preferred.

A man's stationery may be headed

HENRY J. WHITE
40 CLINTON AVENUE
LOS ANGELES 33, CALIFORNIA

The telephone number on either the man's or the woman's stationery may be included with the address or in the upper left corner of the page.

Stationery carrying the crest or monogram of your club, residence hall, or social fraternity is considered good usage among college students. It is often used for invitations to dances, teas, or other social functions sponsored by the group and for Christmas cards from the organization.

Personal stationery bearing your initial or monogram is correct if you are careful to avoid the ostentatious in design and color.

Margins on a letter should be uniform and sufficiently generous to make a neat appearance. Your friends and family will
decipher whatever handwriting they must to learn about you,
but employers are apt to be less patient with illegible and care-
less-looking letters. It is no idle threat that employers actually
give serious consideration to letters that they request "in the
applicant's own handwriting."

INK

The place to try out novel color combinations in paper and
ink is not in social correspondence. Blue, blue-black, and black
are the acceptable colors in ink. Pencil is never used except to
an understanding friend who wouldn't care how the letter
looked just so he heard from you. With ball-point, leakproof
pens as inexpensive and plentiful as they are, almost everyone,
man or woman, keeps a pen always at hand.

In this day and age, when many of us write so poorly that our
friends can scarcely decipher what we have written, it is a boon
to writer and to reader to have a typewriter (with clean type)
used for social correspondence. A typewritten note is acceptable
for social correspondence except in the case of formal invitations and acceptances. Any note that you particularly wish to
personalize, such as a note of sympathy, should be in your own
handwriting.

Envelopes should match the paper and should be of such a
size that the paper fits easily into them when folded. Envelopes
with bright-colored linings are not in good taste for formal correspondence but are acceptable for ordinary social use.

ADDRESSING THE ENVELOPE

The address on the envelope is correctly written with each
line indented slightly and with no punctuation at the ends of
the lines. The name of the addressee should be written out in
full, unless it is too long to fit on the envelope attractively,

when initials may be used. The most important thing is that the address must be legible.

MRS. ADAM MARTIN
17 WALNUT PLACE
CAMBRIDGE 5, MASS.

It is best to write out the name of the state in full, although such long names as Pennsylvania, Massachusetts, District of Columbia, and the like may be abbreviated to Pa., Mass., and D. C.

With the exception of "Mr. and Mrs.," "Messrs.," for unmarried brothers, or "the Misses," for sisters, it is better form to name only one person on the envelope. Any other person or persons may be included in the note by saying "We should like you and your son to come for dinner, etc." The envelope would be more properly addressed "Mrs. James Abrams" than "Mrs. James Abrams and Son."

"Should a letter to a man always be addressed to 'Mr.'?"

An address should include the prefix "Mr." or "Miss" or "Mrs." or a title such as "Dr." or "Professor" if the person has such. Young boys may be addressed as "Master"; and young girls, even children, are always addressed as "Miss."

"What is the proper way to address a letter to a divorced woman?"

A divorced woman usually takes her maiden surname followed by that of her former husband. She becomes Mrs. Woodworth Martin and is so addressed.

According to strictest social usage, a widow retains her husband's name and continues to be "Mrs. Andrew Martin." In actual practice, however, many widows, particularly those who are employed, use their own first names and prefer to be addressed as "Mrs. Grace Martin."

Although a return address on the envelope is not necessary, it is a safeguard. Some correspondents rightly feel it undignified to announce the source of the letter to all eyes. Others feel that onus preferable to having a misaddressed letter posted on a bulletin board under an "IS THIS YOURS?" sign. Postal officials recommend that the name, street, city, zone number, and state of the writer as well as of the addressee appear on all letters, business or social. Business envelopes usually carry return addresses for business reasons.

The Friendly Letter

No one can indicate what should be included in a friendly letter except to suggest that you should not only tell the interesting items about yourself but should remember to comment on the things that your friend has been doing and to take an interest in them. The letter represents you to your friend and he is much more interested in your expressing yourself characteristically and freely than in your following a set of formal rules.

In friendly correspondence between a boy and a girl or a man and a woman, the man takes the initiative both in starting the correspondence and in continuing it. If a woman chooses to disregard this convention, she does so knowing that she is in "Proceed at Your Own Risk" territory.

"Is it proper for a boy to start a correspondence with a girl without previously asking her permission?"

"Should a boy write to a girl before his last letter is answered —cards, Christmas, Valentine, Easter?"

A girl appreciates a young man's asking whether he may write to her, but perhaps the first letter could do double duty—ask permission to start the correspondence and start it! Observance of holidays and special occasions can be made by the exchange of greeting cards between letters.

"How long a time should elapse between getting a letter and answering it?"

To answer immediately is the surest and most interesting way for most of us to handle our correspondence, but it undeniably puts a strain upon the other correspondent. Perhaps setting aside an evening each week or two to reply to letters is advisable in order to space them so that they are neither a boomerang nor a stale accumulation of a month's activities.

The date should appear on every letter. Business letters and often social notes have it under the address, in the upper right-hand corner, in which case it is written "January 3, 19—." Sometimes it is placed at the close of a friendly letter, to the left of the signature. Usually it is then written as "January the third, 19—." Simply "Monday" on a letter or an invitation is correct, but it is confusing and had better be avoided. It could well be Monday, January the third.

"Dear Susan" is an accepted form of salutation for a letter of any degree of intimacy. "My dear Susan" is considered a more formal opening, except in England where the reverse is true. With members of your family or with close friends, other more affectionate salutations are acceptable. A comma is correctly used after the salutation; the colon is correct only in business letters.

THE BODY OF THE LETTER

What you say in your letter to a friend is a matter of personal choice. The form of the letter still remains subject to the usual rules of grammar, punctuation, and sentence construction. Paragraphs are in order in a letter just as they are in any good writing.

A casual reading of the newspapers will convince anyone that he should be careful about the contents of a letter. Pledges of lifelong devotion are worth money in court, and slighting comments about acquaintances often rise later to plague one. No doubt, in his later life, when his political future was dependent in part on Mr. Bryan's support, Woodrow Wilson had occasion to regret many times having written in a letter "Would that we could do something, at once dignified and effective, to knock Mr. Bryan once and for all into a cocked hat."

The forms cordially yours, sincerely yours, most sincerely yours, or very sincerely yours are considered preferable to sincerely or very sincerely. If you wish a more intimate closing, you may say "affectionately yours" or "lovingly yours." "As ever" is safely noncommittal and frequently used. A note signed "hastily" or "hastily yours" is no compliment to your correspondent.

Often the date of the friendly letter, as indicated earlier, appears at the close to the left of the signature.

Except in letters to intimate friends, one's full name should be signed at the letter's close. A parenthetical title may be added in letters to business associates or strangers. For an unmarried woman to use Miss in parenthesis before her name is considered an affectation and bad form by many business and professional women. It seems unnecessary, since a married woman is expected to indicate her married name as shown in the following example:

> *Sincerely yours*
> *Catherine Anderson*
> *(Mrs. Ray Anderson)*

The skeleton form for a friendly letter would appear as follows:

> *William Bowes*
> *981 Bellaire Street*
> *Chicago, Illinois*
>
> *March 24, 19—*

Dear Susan,
           *** ****

> *Sincerely yours,*
> *Bill*

You may have occasion to ask a friend to deliver a note for you. Any letter or note so sent should be left unsealed by the sender and should have "Kindness of Mary Jones" or "Courtesy of John Harris" (the name of the person delivering the note) written on the face of the envelope.

The Thank-you Letter

You are expected to write a thank-you note
1. after you have been a guest overnight
2. after you have received a gift or remembrance of any kind from a friend whom you may not have the opportunity to thank in person
3. after anyone has shown you any particular courtesy, as, for example, after a person in another city has shown you through a school, museum, or other place of interest or in other ways made your stay in the city a pleasant one.

In this third category falls the thank-you note to the faculty members who accommodate groups of students by chaperoning at dances and other affairs, speaking before club meetings, and otherwise giving of their time. While a note may not be required following a dinner party or a small tea, it is a gracious gesture.

The thank-you note or bread-and-butter note is really an abbreviated form of the friendly letter and conforms to the same rules as to salutation and closing. It is sent to the hostess (not jointly to the host and hostess) as soon as possible after your visit is over or after the gift has been received. Excuses such as a "rush of business," "final examinations," or "illness in the family" are not acceptable. You must send the note within a week or be considered lacking in a knowledge of the rudimentary elements of social usage. The hostess is not expected to reply to your note.

The practice that "the woman waits for the man to write the

first letter" has its exception in the case of a young woman's being the guest of a young man, at his home or at college. If you are visiting a friend who lives with his parents, you should write a note to his mother as well as to him. If the mother is not living and the father has taken you to the theater or to a movie, you might say in your letter, "Please tell your father how much I enjoyed going to the theater Wednesday evening."

Individual thank-you notes are necessary from each guest to the host or hostess. It is not correct to write one letter and sign several names. Printed thank-you cards are widely used in acknowledging wedding gifts, flowers for a funeral, or other instances when many notes must be written, but they are undeniably less acceptable to the receiver than a handwritten personal note. If you would be meticulously correct and sincerely wish to express appreciation, you will write your thank-you notes.

Invitations

Invitations, one of the most frequently used forms of social communication, constitute a gracious gesture on the part of the host and a compliment to the guest. It follows that there are responsibilities incumbent upon both participants in the hospitality.

In sending each of the types of invitation, formal and informal, one considers the type of function to which he is inviting guests, and he follows the more or less set rules for the form of the invitation. These established practices will be discussed in the sections that follow.

Most important to remember in replying to invitations is the *necessity of replying* and of *fulfilling your word in going.* "R.S.V.P." (*répondez, s'il vous plaît*—reply, if you please) on an invitation commands your reply, but not always is this or a similar phrase used.

Remember to reply at once to

1. any invitation where the number of guests is a consideration, such as a dinner or a buffet supper
2. any invitation that "requests the pleasure (or honor) of your company." An exception to this general rule is an invitation to a church wedding
3. any invitation that indicates a reply is wanted by including R.S.V.P. on it.

You should experience no difficulty in replying to invitations if you will remember that the answer follows the form of the invitation; that is, an engraved or written invitation requires a written answer that is worded formally or informally depending upon the invitation; a telephoned invitation receives a telephoned reply; and so on. Actually guests sometimes telephone replies to written invitations if they wish to do so. Some written or printed invitations for group functions give the name and telephone number of the person to whom one is expected to reply for the convenience of the recipient of the invitation.

The reply to a formal invitation issued by a man and his wife should be addressed to both Mr. and Mrs. John Smith. The reply to an informal invitation is addressed to the woman only. If several persons are giving a party and no specific one is designated to receive the replies, acknowledgment should be sent to the one at whose home the function is to be held or the one of the group whom you know.

Informal Invitations

Informal friendly invitations are usually written in a style similar to that of the friendly note. Notepaper or a visiting card is used, and often such an invitation is extended by telephone or telegraph. To a telephoned invitation one gives an immediate and definite reply, and to a telegraphed invitation a reply telegram is sent at once.

In issuing an invitation by telephone, the host or hostess

should be specific and complete in the invitation, saying, "Would you like to go with me to hear Bob Jones sing at the Union on Saturday evening?" or "I am having a few friends in to meet my cousin Eleanor Ames on Thursday afternoon at three, and I should like you to come." It is not courteous to ask, "What are you doing Saturday?"

The written informal luncheon or dinner invitation should be sent out a week to two weeks ahead of the date of the function. It should indicate clearly the time of the function. If there is any chance that the guest might be uncertain as to whether formal or informal clothes should be worn, this information should be included. If the hostess is arranging for the transportation of the women guests, she notes her plan in her invitation.

The reply to an informal written invitation should be made at once in writing and should follow, in general, the style of the invitation.

An informal dinner invitation to an unmarried woman might read:

Dear Jane,

I am having a few guests in for dinner at seven next Tuesday, October the nineteenth, and do hope that you can come. I am asking Howard Keller to call for you.

Cordially yours,
Edith Burton

October the ninth

(Informal notes of this sort as well as longer friendly letters may be typewritten or written in longhand as the writer prefers.)

Her reply would be:

Dear Edith,

I shall be delighted to accept your invi-

tation for dinner at seven Tuesday, October
the nineteenth.

It was good of you to arrange for Howard
to call for me. He telephoned today about
coming.

Sincerely yours,
Jane Harmon

October the eleventh

To an unmarried man the hostess might write:

Dear Howard,

I am inviting a few guests for dinner at
seven on Tuesday, October the nineteenth,
and do hope that you can come. Will you please
call for Jane Harmon?

Sincerely yours,
Edith Burton

October the ninth

Howard Keller would reply:

Dear Edith,

Thank you for your nice invitation to dinner at seven on October the nineteenth. I
accept with pleasure and shall be glad to
call for Jane Harmon. I telephoned her this
morning and made arrangements with her.

I am looking forward to the evening with
you.

Sincerely yours,
Howard Keller

October the eleventh

A week-end invitation or any other invitation to a house guest should state clearly the length of time that you wish the guest to remain and the types of clothes that will be needed.

A typical week-end invitation might read:

Dear Catherine,

That week-end party we have talked of is materializing, and we hope that you can be with us for August seventh, eighth, and ninth. There is an informal dance at the Club on Friday, and we hope to have some swimming Saturday.

A train comes in at 4:10 on Friday afternoon, and a bus at 4:40. If you will let us know on which one you will arrive, we will meet you.

It will be a treat to see you again.

                              Affectionately yours,
                                   Helen

July the twenty-first

Visiting cards are often used as invitations to small teas, dances, and suppers. The nature of the function and the time are indicated by a pen notation on the card. Authorities differ widely as to the form the penned words should take, their location on the card, abbreviations, and also the propriety of replying to the invitation by sending one's own visiting card. A satisfactory model invitation would be:

> *To meet Miss Ann Evans*
>
> *Mrs. Ralph Adams Johnson*
>
> *Tuesday, April the ninth*
> *Bridge at two o'clock*

You wouldn't be wrong to send your own card back with "Delighted to come" written in ink above your name, but you would be impeccably correct if you replied on white notepaper with a simple friendly note.

Formal Invitations

To a formal dinner, formal wedding, formal dance, and formal teas and receptions, written or engraved formal invitations are sent. In some instances, new process printed invitations are used. Invitations to such functions should be sent from two to three weeks in advance. If the social event is being sponsored by a club or group the invitation should include the name of the person to whom the reply should be sent.

Custom demands that a particular form be followed in formal invitations and replies, as to both materials used and wording. Cards or plain white sheets of good notepaper are used for formal invitations. Formal invitations are expressed in and must be replied to in the third person.

Occasionally, exception is made to the rule of always issuing formal invitations to formal functions; for instance, some college campuses issue formal dance or dinner invitations personally or by note. The reply in such a case would be in the form of the invitation.

A formal invitation to dinner might be handwritten and read:

> *The Women's Residence Hall Club*
> *requests the pleasure of*
> *Professor and Mrs. Ross Spindler's*
> *company at dinner*
> *in honor of*
> *Distinguished Students*
> *on Monday, the third of May*
> *at seven o'clock*
> *in Shealy Hall*
>
> *Please reply to*
> *Jane Wells*
> *Wood Hall*
> *Telephone 6233*

Very few college groups have their invitations engraved but many do use printed ones if they are issuing a large number of them.

The form might read:

> *The Women's Residence Hall Club*
> *requests the pleasure of your company*
> *at its annual dinner*
> *in honor of*
> *Distinguished Students*
> *on Monday, the third of May*
> *at seven o'clock*
> *in Shealy Hall*

Please reply to
Jane Wells
Wood Hall
Telephone 6233

Social Communication

A formal invitation never is written entirely across the page, in running style, as in an informal invitation. It follows the preceding form and the reply is written in similar form.

The acceptance would read:

Mr. and Mrs. Ross Spindler
accept with pleasure
the kind invitation of
The Women's Residence Hall Club
to dinner
in honor of
Distinguished Students
on Monday, the third of May
at seven o'clock
in Shealy Hall

If it should be necessary to decline an invitation, either formal or informal, it is courteous to explain to one's hostess the reason for declining. The form of the regret should take the form of the invitation. It is not necessary to include the time of the event in a regret, although this item should be included in an acceptance.

A regret would read:

Mr. and Mrs. Ross Spindler
sincerely regret that
they are unable to accept
the kind invitation of
The Women's Residence Hall Club
for dinner
in honor of
Distinguished Students
because of a previous commitment

Unexpected cancellations are the lot of even the best hostesses, and the only thing to be done is to ask a good friend to do you the favor of filling in. If you happen to be the good friend who is thus approached, your feeling should be one of being complimented that you have been considered sensible enough to understand the situation.

Should circumstances make the cancellation of a function necessary, the hostess should send short, written notes at once if there is time to get word to the guests in this way. The form of the recall should be that of the invitation, formal if the invitation was formal, informal if the invitation was such. In an emergency, the telephone would, of course, be used.

Although it is never correct to ask for an invitation for yourself, you might in courtesy to an out-of-town guest ask a hostess if you might bring him to the tea or reception to which you are invited. You do not, however, ask for a luncheon or dinner invitation for a guest; instead, you "regret" the invitation.

"When invited to a special dinner and the invitation does not state whether formal or informal, is it proper to call the hostess to gain such information?"

The form of the invitation usually will tell you what sort of dress you are expected to wear. A formal engraved or printed invitation for a large evening function calls for formal attire for both men and women. Correct formal apparel for a woman is a dinner dress, probably a short ballerina-length one, and for a man a dinner jacket (tuxedo).

If you cannot decide from the invitation what to wear, it is perfectly permissible (and often safer!) to inquire of your hostess. And if any guest asks her, she should by all means accommodate him by replying definitely what sort of dress is expected.

Messages for Special Occasions

Difficult as it sometimes seems to put into words the sympathy that one feels when a death occurs, it is not sufficient to use the printed "sympathy cards" as the easy way out. Any note of condolence should be written on plain white paper in one's own handwriting. A short, simple note, with an offer to be of assistance, is received with appreciation.

A short, handwritten note should be sent as soon as possible after the funeral to those who have shown special courtesy in writing or sending flowers. Printed cards of thanks are sometimes used, but they are not an adequate substitute for a personal handwritten note if you sincerely wish to express your appreciation.

"If a girl's parent dies and the dormitory sends flowers, should the girl on her thank-you note sign her own or her other parent's name?"

The girl should write a note to the group expressing the appreciation of both her family and herself. Her own signature is sufficient, as she will include mention of her parent in the note.

On the occasion of an engagement, a wedding, graduation, or the receipt of some special recognition, short sincere handwritten notes of congratulation to one's friends are to be preferred to the printed card.

In the case of wedding congratulations, one should remember that the groom receives "congratulations" and the bride "best wishes," unless a letter or telegram is sent to the couple jointly, when "congratulations" are correct.

Greeting cards for special occasions like Christmas, birthdays, Easter, or Valentine's Day should express the good wishes of the sender. Christmas cards printed with the sender's name are widely used, but most people still like to receive handwritten messages and signatures.

Chapter Eight

EXTENDING AND RECEIVING COURTESIES

WHAT DO YOU DO IF *you do not know what flowers or what colors a girl would prefer in a corsage? you cannot accept an invitation to a tea? Is a reply necessary? you have to face a receiving line? What are you supposed to say? the person at the head of the receiving line calls you by the wrong name? a boy asks you for a photograph? Does an exchange of photographs have any especial significance?*

ARE YOU EXPECTED TO *wear the corsage sent even though it clashes with your dress? send a gift to the hostess after being a week-end guest? write a thank-you note if you have been a guest for dinner only? send a corsage every time you ask a girl to go to a dance?*

ALL OF US envy those individuals who know how to entertain graciously and who can also accept hospitality in a pleasing manner. Fortunately, both these arts can be cultivated by practice and by intelligent attention to details. Certain definite obligations devolve upon both host and guest.

When you invite a friend to be a guest in your own home, you are extending him one of the choicest courtesies possible. Before he arrives, you will see that the necessary arrangements are made for his comfort. You will pay attention to such details in the guest room as flowers; a new book and a magazine or two; a good reading light; clothes hangers in the closet; and fresh soap, towels, and even a toothbrush in the bathroom.

In this day of small houses, many families do not have a separate guest room. A boy extending an invitation to his room-

158

mate to visit him during the holidays often shares his own room with his guest. A girl who takes a housemate home with her for the week end may do the same. In such instances, the host or hostess will see to it that there is closet room and at least one bureau drawer ready for the guest's belongings.

WHEN THE GUEST ARRIVES

If you know of certain foods that your guest likes especially, a suggestion to your mother will probably bring about the desired result.

As soon as possible after your guest arrives, you will see that he meets the other members of the family. You will arrange for the kind of entertainment that he enjoys and will be responsible for expenses incurred during his visit.

It is the responsibility of the host or hostess to tell the guest the hours at which meals will be served and, if the family and the guest are sharing the same bathroom, to indicate the time when the bathroom will be available. The host should also make the suggestion for retiring. A most awkward situation may arise if both host and guest think it is discourteous to make the first move toward retiring and both sit for hours after they are ready to go to bed.

There is at least one host who always writes a note to his guests thanking them for honoring him by their visit. This would seem to be the ultimate gesture in courtesy.

Responsibilities of the Guest

The guest is careful to arrive at the time when he is expected and not to stay longer than his invitation calls for. He tries to bring with him the personal equipment that he needs so that he will not have to borrow extensively from his host. He is expected to bring his own bathing suit, tennis racket, or tuxedo, if special entertainment requiring such equipment was mentioned in his invitation. He takes an interest in other members of the family besides the particular one whom he is visiting; he is on time for meals; he is careful not to monopolize the bathroom. He observes what the family customs are as to grace before dinner or not smoking in the living room and follows them. In short, he shows consideration for others.

When special entertainment is provided, the gracious guest indicates his appreciation by his enthusiastic participation. If foods that he likes particularly have been prepared for him, he acknowledges this special courtesy. A hostess who has tried hard to please a guest likes to have her efforts noticed. In informal situations, for a guest to refrain from commenting on the efforts of his hostess to please him merely because he has heard that "only a beggar thanks another for food" is straining at the gnat and swallowing the camel. The "good" guest leaves no doubt that he is enjoying his visit.

Many guests like to bring a small gift to their host or hostess or their friend's mother. Books, magazines, candy, and flowers are always acceptable and may be delivered in person or sent after the visit is over.

THE THANK-YOU NOTE

One "must" for the guest is that he send a thank-you note both to his host and to his host's mother as soon as possible after his visit has been completed. Examinations, minor illness, or extra work is not an adequate excuse for failing to observe this courtesy of guest to host. A person who is a guest for luncheon or dinner only need not write a thank-you note but does thank his friend and his friend's mother before leaving.

A guest tries to return a friend's hospitality. It is not necessary that he return it in kind, but he will at a later date invite his host to the theater, a concert, dinner, or a movie or in some other way show that he has not forgotten the courtesy extended him.

Entertaining a Guest on Campus

Many questions have to be settled with regard to entertaining an out-of-town guest at college, whether a man is entertaining a girl or a girl entertaining a man. If a man invites a girl to the campus for the week end, should he pay for her room? How about the meals? Does he pay for her railroad ticket? Is it all right for her to stay in a reputable hotel without chaperonage? If a girl invites a man from off campus to come for a football game or residence hall dance, what financial responsibility does she carry?

Answers to these questions:

"If a boy asks a girl to come to the campus for a social event should he pay all of her expenses?"

"If a girl asks a boy to come to the campus for a social event should she pay all expenses?"

by campus leaders indicate that more expenses are borne by men hosts than by women who invite guests. The great majority of men hosts apparently pay all expenses except transportation incurred by girls' coming to campus as their guests. A woman playing hostess, however, seems to carry little expense excepting the cost of the social event itself.

If a man is playing host to an off-campus girl—"importing" in the language of the campus—he plans the details of the visit carefully. One thing of particular concern to her parents and to the college authorities, both of her own school, if she happens to be a student elsewhere, and to those of the school where she is visiting, is where she will stay. The man makes arrangements for this well in advance.

Most colleges have some facilities for housing out-of-town guests, such as a lodge run in connection with the college or a union building on the campus. Where these accommodations are not available, there are often places in some of the clubs, sororities, or residence halls. A man does not usually take his campus visitor to a hotel. If she is in college elsewhere, her college probably has regulations requiring that she stay in a college house. With whatever organization she may stay she should observe without question college and house regulations, not only because common courtesy demands it but because, if she takes advantage of her position as a guest to ignore regulations, houses will be much less willing to accommodate other out-of-town guests for later functions.

Sometimes a man asks a girl on campus whom he knows to act as hostess for his guest and entertain the guest in her own room. A man should realize that, if the girls do not know one another, he is straining to the limit the good will of both. He should consider carefully before he asks a girl to share her room with another girl who is a total stranger.

In most coeducational schools, when a girl invites a man to the campus for a house dance or a football game, she pays only the cost of the ticket. He pays for transportation, meals, and entertainment other than the event for which he was invited. In some of the women's colleges, the hostess pays all the expenses after the man reaches the campus. If the man stays in one of the college houses it is customary for the girl to pay the cost, but if he stays in a hotel, he pays his own bill. For important dances of the year men sometimes move out of their houses and turn them over to the girls for the week end—such arrangements can be advantageous in terms of both cost and fun if the group plans carefully with the full cooperation of the college officials as to chaperons, hours for visiting in the house, and so on.

Group Entertaining on Campus

Much of the entertaining at college is done by student groups —clubs, fraternities, sororities, residence halls, cooperatives.

Group functions are usually dinners, dances, teas, or receptions. It is the responsibility of the social chairman to schedule these events in the college office and to obtain approval of the arrangements made for them.

Groups give dinners both for student and for faculty groups. One of the popular dinners is the exchange, or "trade," dinner at which a men's group entertains a women's group as a group affair, or vice versa. Sometimes the arrangement is that half the men's group go to the girls' house and half the girls to the men's house. In such instances, the men and the girls who stay in their own houses are hosts and hostesses, respectively, and are responsible for making the affair a success. Men's groups are expected to furnish chaperonage in their house, just as girls' groups do for the functions at which men are their guests. Some planning in advance is necessary by the social committee in charge in order to make these affairs run smoothly.

When faculty members are entertained, it is common practice to arrange for individual students within the group to be responsible for particular faculty guests. This plan works well enough if other members of the group do not therefore feel that they are released from all responsibility in making faculty guests feel at home. Every member of the group should feel responsible for talking briefly with at least one faculty member to whom he is not assigned, before or after dinner.

DANCES

The responsibility of the group giving a dance does not end with engaging an orchestra and issuing invitations. The responsibility for the conduct of the dance rests with the organization itself, not with faculty guests, chaperons, sponsors, or other adults whose position at the dance should be that of honor guests, not policemen.

Invitations, including those to faculty guests and chaperons, should be sent two weeks in advance of the date of the event.

For most large group functions, invitations are written, engraved, or printed.

Neglect of faculty guests at dances has become so marked on some campuses that it is difficult to persuade faculty members to attend student functions. Their objection usually is not that they find themselves with unpleasant responsibilities; it is rather that they are ignored completely, meet few students, and spend the evening being badly bored.

When the faculty guests arrive, each member of the social committee should speak to them and should introduce his companion. The same procedure should be followed when a girls' group is entertaining. If the dance is a small one, each member of the group should feel it his personal responsibility to chat for a few minutes with the guests. If the man does not suggest speaking to the sponsors, the girl should do so. Dances should be exchanged if the faculty guests are dancing. Some groups have solved the problem of showing faculty guests that they appreciate their coming by scheduling a fifteen minute to half hour reception for them in the middle of the evening. Students then know exactly when and where they may pay their respects to their faculty friends, and find it easy to do so. Faculty in turn have the opportunity to meet and visit informally with several students at least, and this is usually their main objective in attending student parties. In short, if faculty guests are invited, the group should make a definite effort to see that they feel welcome and to have them leave with the feeling that the group appreciated their coming.

TEAS

Teas are one of the favorite means of entertainment on college campuses. There are teas for new students, teas for distinguished visitors, teas for the faculty, teas for rushees, teas for other social groups, and teas in honor of new head residents and housemothers. In fact, teas are as much a part of campus life as chemistry classes or football games.

Written, printed, or engraved invitations should be sent from ten days to two weeks before the date of the function. The invitation may read

---

ALPHA MU

OF

GAMMA GAMMA GAMMA

Sunday, March the fourth   *128 Grant Street*

Four to Six

---

or, more formally,

The Cary Club

requests the pleasure of your company
on Sunday, the fourth of March
from four until six o'clock
in Cary Hall East
140 Stadium Avenue

At the same time that invitations are issued, certain special friends of the group—sponsors, faculty members, alumnae, or townspeople—will be asked to pour. The usual time for one individual to pour is thirty minutes.

It is not necessary to reply to an invitation to a large tea. When one organization invites official representatives of another, someone from the group should attend. Faculty members often send informal notes when they are unable to accept a tea invitation.

Street-length dresses are always in good taste at afternoon teas, both for the hostess group and for the guests. Women guests wear afternoon dresses or costume suits, hats, and gloves and usually carry handbags. Men wear business suits, either receiving or calling.

At a smart tea, care is taken not to overload the table; refreshments are kept simple. In fact, one might almost say, the simpler the refreshments the smarter the tea. The primary purpose of the refreshments, aside from the gesture of hospitality, is to appeal to the caller's aesthetic sense, not to satisfy his hunger. Tea and coffee, or fruit punch in warm weather, sandwiches and small cakes (preferably not sticky ones), and mints and nuts are more or less standard refreshments. It is not necessary to serve all these, however.

Before the guests arrive, a final check should be made to see that

1. the guest room or cloak room is in order, with the bed clear to receive wraps (or hangers provided for them).
2. a mirror, full length if possible, is close at hand.
3. soap and guest towels are in the guest bathroom.
4. the refreshment table is in order, and replacements and details of serving are understood by the serving and kitchen assistants.

Careful plans for receiving guests should be made by the social chairman. He should see that

1. several individuals are in the living room ready to receive guests at least thirty minutes before the time stated in the invitation. Attention to this important item may prevent embarrassing moments both for the receiving group and for the guest whose watch is fast. All others on duty at the

beginning of the tea should be ready at least ten minutes early.

2. a student who knows a large number of the guests is detailed to open the door and greet them, and another to introduce guests to the person at the head of the receiving line.

3. members of the group are in the hall to show guests to the cloak room.

4. guests are met at the end of the receiving line, introduced to other guests, and shown items of interest in the house before being taken to the dining room.

The receiving line is merely a useful device for enabling guests to meet easily the officers of the group, the guest of honor, the house director, and selected members of the group. The order in line is usually: the president of the group; the house director; the guest of honor; the group adviser; and, if desired, other student officers and sponsors. The guest should give his name to the person standing near the head of the line whose function it is to introduce him to the first person in the line. The guest says, "How do you do?" adding the person's name if he chooses, to each one in the line.

Introductions in a receiving line follow, in general, the same order as in any other situation. That is, a man coming down the line would be introduced to a woman in the line; but a man in the line would be introduced to a woman coming down the line, unless he were a man of eminence. Where there is no distinction of age or sex, the person coming down the line is introduced to the persons in line.

It is the responsibility of each person in the line to repeat clearly the name of the guest to the next person in line. If a guest's name is garbled, the guest himself is at perfect liberty to correct the error.

At most teas, a guest is expected to help himself to refreshments other than the tea or coffee. When student groups entertain, they usually have enough members so that the individual host or hostess can seat the guest in the dining room and serve him or see that one of the assistants in the dining room does so.

The student host or hostess sees that the guest gets his wraps and goes with him to the door. If guests are still arriving, it is not at all necessary for the guest to say good-by to the head of the receiving line. If the person at the head of the line is free, he may very properly express appreciation for the courtesy shown him.

Receptions are similar both in form and in purpose to teas. An afternoon reception differs in no essential way from an afternoon tea. An evening reception is usually formal and is often followed by dancing. The techniques used for teas hold equally well for receptions.

"When does one remove her gloves at a tea—on entering the room or just before being served?"

A woman removes her gloves when she is served. She may remove one or both sooner if she wishes to.

"Do you unfold your napkin at a tea all the way, halfway, or not at all?"

Very small paper napkins are commonly used for this type of entertaining. One usually unfolds a small napkin of this sort halfway.

"What is the correct length of time to remain at a tea?"

The length of time to stay at a tea depends somewhat upon the circumstances, but usually twenty minutes to half an hour should be satisfactory to both host and guest.

"Should the gentleman or the lady suggest that the couple leave the reception?"

When a man and woman attend a tea or reception together, it is the woman's place to make the first move to go. The man follows her lead immediately.

Small Courtesies

Flowers may be termed the universal gift. They are suitable for such joyful events as weddings, dances, birthdays, anniversaries, initiations, births, graduations, and Christmas. They are equally suitable as expressions of sympathy.

One of the small courtesies extended most frequently by young men to girls is that of sending a corsage for a special dance. Corsages are not expected for college mixers, tea dances, or other informal dances but only on such occasions as the junior prom, the sophomore cotillion, the girl's sorority or residence-hall dance, the men's club, hall, or fraternity formal. Many campuses have their own traditions about sending corsages, and some student groups rule that corsages are not to be sent because of the additional expense involved.

The choice of colors and flower combinations rests, of course, with the man. He usually tries to find out from the roommate of the girl whom he is taking to the dance the color of the dress that she is to wear. If he cannot find out in any other way, he should ask the girl herself rather than take a chance on ruining her ensemble. There is nothing amiss about asking the girl what color flowers she prefers; it is only considered subtler to find out some other way. Having this information at hand, the man must decide for himself whether he wishes to make his own selection of flowers or leave the matter to the judgment of the florist.

It is acceptable for the man to bring the corsage when he comes or he may send it ahead to give the girl an opportunity to adjust it before he arrives.

"Upon receiving a corsage that definitely clashes with one's formal, what does one do?"

"Is it necessary to wear a corsage, if one is given you, if you don't care for it?"

Not only *may* flowers be accepted when they are sent; they *must* be accepted from one who has gone to the trouble and expense of sending them for a special occasion. If you think that you simply cannot combine the flowers with the dress that you had intended to wear, change either your dress or the position of the flowers, putting them in your hair or on your wrist where they won't cause so violent a contrast. A bizarre color combination is to be preferred to hurting the feelings of the man who has meant to give you pleasure.

The matter of *when* a girl thanks a young man for a corsage would seem to depend upon the particular circumstances of the evening. She will do so as soon as they have a few moments of privacy. A young man likes to know as soon as possible whether he has succeeded in pleasing a girl in his careful selection.

The usual corsage is made to be worn on the shoulder. Some, however, are to be worn in the hair or on the wrist. A girl can judge from the size and structure of the corsage the position most suitable for it. Left shoulder seems to be preferred to right shoulder, but the choice is the individual's. In general, flowers are placed heads up as they grow naturally.

Gifts

Choosing gifts for other people is one of the genuine pleasures of life, especially if one has a good idea in mind. One's originality, or the lack of it, is nowhere more clearly shown than in his choice of gifts. The thought behind the gift is as important to the recipient as the gift itself. It is a matter of common observation that we tend to buy for others the things that we want for ourselves. The old story about the man who gave his wife an air rifle for Christmas after she had presented him with a living-room chair for his birthday has its modern counterparts. The ideal gift is one that pleases both the donor and the recipient; but if a choice must be made, the recipient comes first.

> "*What kind of gifts should a girl accept from a boy she is not engaged to?*"
>
> "*How well should a girl know a boy before she gives him her photograph?*"
>
> "*What is a general suggestion for a girl's birthday present?*"

If a man is engaged to a girl, he may with propriety give her personal and expensive gifts. Otherwise, he bestows lingerie and jewelry sparingly and money never. Likewise, a girl is conservative in her gifts to a man. Men are said to prefer to choose their own neckties and socks, but they seem to take considerable pleasure and pride in the hand-knit articles that their girls make for them.

There is a wide difference of opinion as to the suitability of a man and a girl who are not engaged exchanging photographs. If either decides to give a photograph to the other, it would be well not to inscribe a pledge of eternal devotion across the corner.

There can be no "general suggestion" for a gift for a girl other than the standard formula of candy-books-flowers. A gift is not general; it is particular. If a man knows a girl's tastes and interests, he should be able to please her with a gift. Whether one acknowledges a courtesy by a gift or only by a note is not so important as the fact that one must acknowledge it.

Promptness is the most important item in acknowledging a gift. Whether the acknowledgment is made in writing or in person depends upon individual considerations.

The Little Foxes

The little foxes, that spoil the vines.—Song of Solomon

These small courtesies may not be disregarded:

1. A man rises when a woman enters or leaves a room and remains standing as long as she is standing. A young woman rises for older women.
2. A person who is speaking may not be interrupted.
3. Another's mail is inviolate—whether or not the letter has previously been opened.
4. Whenever there is a choice, one walks behind, not in front of, other people. If there is no choice, he excuses himself for crossing in front of them.
5. Any service, however slight, is acknowledged with a "thank you," whether or not one has paid for it.
6. The formula "Excuse me, please," applies when one touches another person inadvertently, interrupts anyone, hiccups, or in any other way inconveniences or offends others.
7. The door to another's office, home, or room is private. Before entering, one should knock and wait to be invited to come in.

On campus, the following courtesies are important:

1. Speaking to professors, to the president, and to other administrative officers, whether or not they know you personally.
2. Rising when a professor enters his office. Girls, as well as men, may well observe this courtesy.
3. Remaining standing in a private office until you are invited to be seated. Don't ask to smoke; let the invitation come from the professor.
4. Gum chewing in classes, during business hours if you are dealing with people, and at social functions, above all at formal dances, is the last word in bad form.
5. Girls, as well as men, rise when a woman faculty member,

housemother, or head resident joins or leaves a group. Men observe the same courtesy for men faculty members.

6. Your visitor is introduced to the professor whose class he is visiting.

7. Other people's privacy should be respected—your housemates' and your roommate's as well.

Chapter Nine

TRAVEL

DO YOU KNOW *the difference between European-plan and American-plan hotel rates? where to turn to get expert help in planning a short trip by car or an extended vacation in Europe? the best time to inquire about your table assignment on shipboard? when to countersign a traveler's check?*

DO YOU KNOW WHETHER OR NOT *a hotel is usually willing to show you rooms before you engage one? you use the title "Miss" when you register at a hotel?*

DO YOU KNOW WHAT THE MINIMUM ACCEPTABLE TIP IS FOR *a bellboy who delivers a telegram to your hotel room? a waiter if your bill is two dollars? a taxi driver if your fare is seventy-five cents? the service-staff members on a ship?*

DO YOU *"share expenses" of a car by buying half the gas? carry away silver teaspoons or towels as souvenirs of the hotel in which you have been a guest?*

THE ANTICIPATION AND PLANNING of a trip can be half the fun. Travel bureaus render such complete service that all you have to do is to tell them how long a vacation you have and how much money you can afford to spend, and they will be ready with numerous suggestions of where to go, how to get there, where to stay, and what to do. Their services are available *without charge* to you as a prospective traveler, regardless of the amount of business that your particular trip may involve. The travel sections of the Sunday *New York Times* and those of many other newspapers as well always contain the names of innumerable organizations of this sort. More than likely there is at least a small travel bureau in your own city that is well stocked with fascinating travel folders and staffed by an experienced traveler. Travel-bureau personnel know in detail how to handle the physical arrangements of travel outside the United States. But more than that they can also give you some pertinent hints on how to serve your country well and be more popular yourself while traveling in a foreign country. In the long run this information and attention to it on your part may well turn out to be the most important part of your trip.

Vera Micheles Dean, a well-known editor of the Foreign Policy Association, made this point effectively in a talk to several hundred college students on one of our Middle Western campuses during a vocational conference. Speaking from her extensive experience and background in foreign affairs, she stressed that the first and most important job for all of us is to make friends for the United States. Our own State Department considers this matter so important that it sends out material to all persons who obtain passports and visas mentioning some of the things that all of us can do when we travel, so that we really will serve as ambassadors of good will for our country. It is important, when visiting another country, to travel with an open mind, trying to appreciate and enjoy, rather than to disparage and deprecate, the ways in which that country's customs differ from those we are accustomed to. British ice cream may be thin and watery, but their Devonshire clotted cream puts our whipped cream to shame.

Among the services a travel bureau can give you is information about the passports and visas you will require. You will want to make application for these several months in advance of your need for them, so early planning will be to your advantage.

ADVANCE RESERVATIONS

Advance reservations either for transportation or for overnight accommodations are a necessity in most instances and a convenience in any case. A travel agency will gladly make these reservations for you, or you may make them direct if you know exactly what you want. In arranging for transportation, it is advisable to ask the price of a round-trip ticket, which may nearly always be purchased at a considerable reduction over two one-way fares.

Your luggage, as well as your own appearance, represents you to your fellow travelers, so neatness is worth striving for. An experienced traveler knows that he is apt to want to take along more clothes and equipment than he really needs, so he tries to visualize exactly what he requires and to pack accordingly. Heavy luggage may, of course, be checked through on your ticket to your destination by having it delivered to the baggage room and presenting your ticket to the baggage-room attendant with instructions. Your hand luggage should contain all of the necessities that you will need en route. It is well to remember that there are usually restrictions on the weight of the baggage that may be carried without extra charge. Many foreign railways have added restrictions on its size. Steamer suitcases and steamer trunks which can be carried in a taxi often save transfer charges and delay as well. If you are planning to travel by airplane, lightweight luggage is essential.

TRAVELER'S CHECKS

Traveler's checks offer a good solution to the problem of carrying too much cash and are a necessity for foreign travel. One variety of them may be obtained from the American Express company in various denominations; they are readily convertible into cash by countersigning them in the presence of the person to whom you are presenting them as payment. Your signature affixed in his presence is his guarantee that they belong to you. Don't try to be forehanded by countersigning them before you wish to cash them!

A background of knowledge concerning the part of the country in which you are traveling or the points of interest that you may see will add considerably to your enjoyment. Experienced travelers are emphatic in asserting that you get out of a trip what you put into it before you go. In other words, part of the trip is the study that you do before you start. Every year a spate of new travel books appears from which the prospective traveler may choose.

MAPS

Maps are a stimulant to your anticipation of the trip, a source of practical information during it, and a treasured memento long afterward. Acknowledgment is here made to the commercial oil companies of the United States and to the State Highway Commissions of many states for their generous provision of free maps and touring aids. Most of the large oil companies will route a motor trip for you carefully to any place in this country or Canada and supply you with detailed maps and historical information about the country and towns through which you will pass. We are apt to take this service very much for granted because it is so freely given, but you will find road maps somewhat scarce and expensive in most other countries.

The American Automobile Association or Triple A, as it is often called, provides its members with a variety of services including listings of standard hotels, motels, restaurants, road information, weather information, advance reservations, and a certain amount of road service to your car.

Many persons prefer to join a tour group rather than to set forth alone on an expedition. Investigation of such possibilities through your travel bureau or, in the case of students, through the International Travel Office of the United States National Student Association will give you information regarding tours arranged for many special-interest groups. Your college registrar or personnel office will have information available about joint study-travel programs with groups of congenial people.

By Train

In this age of automobiles, college men going on trips with the team or girls attending student conferences away from their own campus may find themselves on a train literally for the first time in their lives. In order to make the most fun out of your trip, you will want to take advantage of the many services available to you.

A redcap is almost a necessity, as a guide as well as a porter, in any large station, particularly if the station is new to you. Not only will he steer you safely through the maze of tunnels, but he may be trusted to deliver your luggage safely to your seat in the train if you have a reservation in a Pullman, parlor car, or reserved-seat coach. If your train does not have reserved-seat coaches, then let the redcap take your bags and find a seat for you. The girl who asks, "If one really can't afford to tip the porter, should one carry her own bag, or is this a service that must be used?" certainly need have no qualms about carrying her own bag if she is physically able to manage it. A redcap can always be refused with a "Thank you very much, but I'll carry it myself." He may look grieved, but not half so much as he will if you let him carry the bag and then don't pay him for his services.

WHICH SEAT

If your Pullman reservation is for a lower berth, you are entitled to the seat that faces forward; if you have the upper one, your seat faces backward. Coach seats on many trains are now reserved for a small fee and reservations must be made in advance.

It is vital to get a check at the time you surrender your luggage and helpful to note the number the porter wears on his cap. If you do not get a check, you have no claim on your luggage. In most stations there is a standard fee fixed by the railroad for each bag or parcel carried. These fees are usually posted in conspicuous places. In addition to the standard fee you are expected to give the redcap a tip of ten cents a bag for one or two bags or a quarter for assorted luggage. It is considerate to tip when you surrender your bags to him unless you are going to stay right with him and your bags yourself.

The Pullman porter will arrange your luggage for you, supply you with a paper hat bag, bring you a pillow or card table if you ask him, brush your clothes, and otherwise attend to your comforts. At night, he will make up your berth while you make your nightly ablutions in the dressing room at the end of the car. If yours is the upper berth, he will bring a ladder for your convenience in climbing up to it for the night.

Berths are somewhat cramped quarters at best, but it is better to do as much dressing and undressing in them as possible. They do have the advantage of privacy, which is more than can be said of the dressing room during rush hours. For a charge slightly more than that for a lower berth on many trains you can obtain a roomette. This accommodation gives you complete privacy and contains wash bowl and toilet facilities.

Parlor-car seats for daytime travel are available to first-class ticket holders for a charge somewhat less than the charge for a lower berth for night travel for a corresponding distance. The newer streamlined coaches with reclining seats, obtainable through advance reservations, are so convenient and comfortable that many experienced travelers use them for both day and night travel and so gain the advantage of coach fare, which is always less than first-class fare required for use of Pullman space.

DINING CAR

Eating in the dining car is a major pleasure of a train trip on many railroads. À la carte (ordering items separately) and table d'hôte (the entire dinner for a set price) service will no doubt both be offered, and you may choose what you will eat according to your inclination and your pocketbook. This service is available to both Pullman and coach passengers.

Most through trains also offer lunch service in the coaches, handled by someone who peddles sandwiches and coffee at mealtimes, or they operate a snack bar where the service is less elegant than in the dining car and the food prices are lower.

STRANGERS

"If, when traveling, a stranger on the train offers to pay for your meal, what should you do?"

The matter of being too friendly with strangers deserves some consideration, for girls traveling alone can get themselves into embarrassing situations without meaning to. It may sound old-fashioned, but it's pretty good sense to keep any acquaintance that you may make in such a situation on an entirely impersonal basis and not obligate yourself in any way by accepting favors. You will do better by paying for your own meal while acknowledging the offer with a courteous, "I'll take care of it, thank you."

Most strangers mean well, but some do not. If you've been talking with a stranger, you may find yourself being showered with advice and offers of assistance. Bona fide employees of the railway are your best source of information, and regularly licensed taxicabs are to be preferred to any rides offered by strangers.

When you are not eating or sleeping or resting, you may want to wander through the train to the observation or lounge car. This is usually at the rear of the train, but the porter will know exactly where it is if you can't find it. If this car is carried, its use is always available to first-class Pullman and parlor-car passengers but not always to coach passengers. On the de luxe coach trains there is usually a lounge car especially for coach passengers. This may be combined with the snack bar. If you question whether or not any facilities are available to you, don't hesitate to ask any member of the train staff for the information that you need.

The matter of tips for services rendered you on a train is treated in the last section of this chapter, which is devoted to the general subject of tipping.

By Ship

Most people have the fun of traveling by ship even less often than they do by train. Your travel agent can make such arrangements for you as table and deck-chair assignments ahead of time if you request them; you will have a choice of early or late sittings at table and some choice of location for your deck chair. You should check with the stewards in charge of these services immediately upon embarking, however, to confirm your reservation. You will also need to find the bath steward and get a schedule for your daily bath unless the particular ship you are on has a generous number of bath facilities available.

Unless you are traveling with companions, you will doubtless find yourself sharing a cabin with one or more strangers. Because you are in a fairly crowded space at best, you should be doubly meticulous about keeping your belongings in order and not usurping more than your fair share of luggage or wardrobe space. May your cabin mates return the compliment.

On shipboard, you are expected to greet ship's officers and persons whom you have passed often in your wanderings around deck with a civil "good morning," whether or not you have been introduced. You will, if you are like most people, enjoy your trip more if you find interesting persons to chat with occasionally, so don't feel obliged to maintain too stony a silence. On the other hand, you have probably been warned often enough about being too forward and will not offend on that score.

DRESS

The size of your ship and the class of your passage will influence whether or not you dress for dinner. In any case, you will probably change your clothing from that worn for lounging around on deck all day. Details of clothing suitable for shipboard will be found in the chapter on Personal Appearance; also, most advertising folders for cruises distributed by travel agencies will give you an idea of the sort of clothing that your particular trip will require.

The matter of tipping the various employees of the ship for their services is discussed in the general section on tipping at the end of the present chapter.

By Plane

Plane travel is to many people the most thrilling mode of transportation. Most trips are of such short duration that few problems arise, but with world-wide travel by air increasing tremendously, some thought needs to be given to your requirements on a longer trip. Certainly if you plan to be on the plane overnight, you will want to carry the essential toilet articles with you in handbag or brief case.

Complimentary meals are served on nearly all flights, except domestic tourist or aircoach ones, that are in progress during a normal meal hour. Meals are also served on international tourist flights. Your timetable will show whether a meal is to be served if you need the information for your planning.

The stewardesses on planes are well-trained in looking after your needs and comforts. They are familiar with first-aid routines as well as the art of being a hostess and will take pride in serving you if you will let your needs be known. Airline personnel are not tipped for their services. The only exception is the sky-cap who handles your luggage. Tipping is not required here, but is expected.

By Car

Many persons today are far more familiar with the techniques of travel by automobile than they are with those for travel by train, plane, or ship. If you are driving your own or another's car, the requirements of driver's license, insurance, and traffic regulations of the state must be checked, if you would enjoy peace of mind and comparative ease of conscience, especially in case of an accident. Enough energy is burned up impatiently waiting for red lights to turn green to reform the world, yet everyone recognizes the necessity of traffic regulations. A philosophical point of view about a thirty-second delay and a determination not to be goaded into taking a foolish chance by irritating drivers ahead of or following you will help make car driving a relaxation rather than a wasteful outpouring of nervous energy. Americans probably need to learn to take it easy on the road more than anywhere else.

If you are riding in another's car, you should have a fairly clear notion of what it costs per mile to operate a car in order that you may share expenses intelligently. Gasoline and oil are, in reality, only a small part of the expense. There are taxes, insurance, license plates, greasing, repairs, and depreciation in addition. An equitable distribution of cost among passengers will show recognition of what the owner is contributing by furnishing the car.

As a passenger, you have an obligation to accede gracefully to the choice of the owner in stopping for meals or overnight. If you would be a popular passenger, you will be considerate about drafts and smoking and not always have to sit in the choice seats by the windows or beside the driver. And one mark of the experienced traveler is his or her ability to assemble essential clothing and equipment into a minimum amount of luggage. A long drive makes people edgy before they know it, so any contribution that you can make by being your most cheerful and accommodating self will probably be appreciated by all other occupants of the car.

Hotel Accommodations

Hotel accommodations may vary all the way from the most elaborate ones in big cities and fashionable resorts to the overnight motel or auto court, which is being used increasingly by the automobile tourist. Most hotels in this country quote rates on the so-called European plan, which means rooms only, no meals included. Frequently, resort hotels quote rates on the American plan, which means that the regular three daily meals are included as well as the room.

The business of procuring the sort of room that you wish at approximately the rate that you wish to pay is sometimes a matter of letting the room clerk know as clearly as possible what you do want. You are within your rights if you inquire from the room clerk about the range of rates, location of rooms, and what facilities are available at the different price levels. If you are traveling on a limited budget, your cue is to inquire about a minimum-rate room. The desk clerk in a large metropolitan hotel might look askance if you asked to see the room before you engaged it, but if you have made some inquiries before going to your room and then find it unsatisfactory upon arrival, it is not out of order to inquire if anything else is available. In out-of-the-way places and in unfamiliar small hotels you are well-advised to look at the room before moving in all of your luggage.

RESERVATIONS

Advance reservations for hotel accommodations are a great convenience during busy seasons. They will do much to assure you of a minimum-rate room, if that is what you need, and will otherwise smooth your path upon arrival. There are types of telegraph service, not particularly well known, by which travelers may wire for reservations or keep friends and relatives informed of their whereabouts at less than the straight-message rate. Any telegraph office will give you full details. Most of the hotel chains maintain free reservation service from one city to another, and there are firms of hotel representatives that make reservations without charge for the particular hotels they represent.

"How does a woman register at a hotel?"

The correct registrations for travelers are

Man: Henry Fellows—Complete address
Man and wife: Mr. and Mrs. Henry Fellows—Complete address
Married woman (*or widow*): Mrs. Henry Fellows—Complete address
Single woman: Nancy Fellows—Complete address
Any child: Henry Fellows, Jr.—Complete address—or Sally Fellows—Complete address

You are expected to tell the clerk at the time when you register how long you will be staying.

The clerk with whom you register will give the key to a bellboy, who in turn will carry your bags and lead you to your room. The boy will also be glad to serve you in any further way, such as bringing you ice water or a newspaper or taking care of any other errands that you may ask him to do. He will expect a tip.

The hotel telephone operator will connect you with the proper department responsible for any of the many services offered by the hotel. She will know whom to call for more towels, a meal in your room, the best information about sightseeing trips, an electric fan, or almost anything else you may need.

Most hotels caution you to keep your room locked at all times and to deposit any large amount of money or valuables in the office safe. If you value your privacy and your valuables, you should follow their advice.

There are some guest obligations in a hotel that, if followed, would greatly cheer the life of the hotel management. It is no small job of housekeeping to keep hundreds of rooms and their equipment in good order. A guest who is careful about where he drops his chewing gum, cigarette ashes, and stubs; who recognizes that ash trays, table silver, and towels and other linen *belong* to the hotel and are not meant for souvenirs; and who uses a shoe cloth instead of a good linen towel on his shoes is a much more welcome guest than one who disregards these items.

YOUR BILL

Shortly before you are ready to leave, you should telephone the desk and ask that your bill be prepared and that a boy be sent up for your luggage. In many auto courts and tourist homes, it is customary to pay when you register, especially if you plan to leave early in the morning.

Tipping

Although many people regard tipping as highly undesirable and consider it contrary to a democratic philosophy, the practice is well-nigh universal. You not only have to know (or guess) how much to tip in an infinite variety of situations, but you have to know whom to tip—and, equally important, who is never tipped. Little as we may like the custom, both because of the principle involved and the uncertainties inherent in it, unless we are prepared to brave the wrath of the untipped, we might as well accede gracefully. One business woman we know says she always figures what she believes to be a reasonable amount for the tip when she is paying her bill and then reaches into a special pocket for an extra quarter. It has almost reached the point where only the tip on top of the tip is recognized pleasantly by some recipients. Be that as it may, you have to know the answers to such questions as these and act accordingly, if you would preserve unruffled tempers:

"How much should a waiter be tipped, and when?"

"Should one leave a tip when one pays the cashier oneself?"

"How much should one give a redcap or a bellboy for carrying one's bags?"

"How do you know how much to tip a taxi driver?"

"What tip should be given a bellboy who delivers a telegram to one's room?"

"How much should a man pay the attendant who checks his hat and coat?"

"What is the correct tip for a Pullman porter on an overnight trip?"

"How much should one tip a hairdresser on a small bill?"

There are two so-called general rules with regard to tipping with enough "buts" and "excepts" tacked on that they can hardly be called general rules:

1. When a definite bill is involved, such as a restaurant check, a hairdresser's bill, or taxi fare, the usual tip is 15 per cent plus. If the service is particularly good or you have required special service, you are expected to increase your tip.

2. If no definite bill is involved, as, for instance, when a redcap carries your bags or a bellboy delivers a telegram, then you tip in proportion to the amount of service rendered.

But if a waiter has served more than one person, his tip would be at least fifteen to twenty cents per person on a small check. On a large check if 15 per cent would be more than $2.00 then the tip could be reduced to 10 per cent. If you pay the waiter directly and he returns the change on a little tray, then you leave the tip on that. If you pay the cashier yourself, then you leave the tip on the table inconspicuously under the edge of your plate.

A hairdresser's or barber's tip runs about a quarter for one service or 15 per cent for a larger bill, but you need not tip at all if the person who has served you is the owner or manager of the place.

A taxi driver expects 15 per cent for a long trip but more in proportion for short runs. He expects nothing less than a total of fifty cents (fare plus tip) no matter how short the trip.

A bellboy or porter who carries your bags and escorts you to your hotel room or helps you when you check out gets twenty-five cents as a minimum and more in proportion to the amount of luggage he takes care of. If he brings a telegram, special-delivery letter, or package to your room, the tip is fifteen or twenty-five cents. The tipping of hotel employees is somewhat in proportion to the general level of cost in the hotel. The doorman at the hotel looks for a tip of twenty-five cents if he calls a cab for you and for more if he lets you leave your car near the entrance for a short time or takes care of having it garaged for you.

The expected tip from a man for checking his hat and coat varies somewhat also with the cost level of the restaurant. Twenty-five cents covers practically any check room but you might give fifteen cents for a hat only or at a less expensive place.

Attendants in both men's and women's washrooms get fifteen to twenty-five cents for a towel, a quick brush, and maybe a spot of hand lotion.

A Pullman porter expects fifty cents to a dollar for an overnight trip.

The maid who takes care of your room in a commercial hotel frequently is not tipped if you are there for a very short stay, but if you are there for four or five days you would probably give her a dollar. At resort hotels it is customary to tip the maids when you leave and the expected amount is at the rate of approximately fifty cents per day.

TIPPING ON SHIPBOARD

On shipboard, there are tips of all kinds to be bestowed, usually at the end of the voyage, unless the cruise is a long one, when tipping is done weekly. The accepted practice among students, college professors, and others of modest means is to decide on the total amount that they can afford for tips and then distribute this amount among the bath steward, the table steward, the deck steward, the room steward, and the stewardess, according to the service each has rendered. The room and the table stewards are normally given larger tips than the deck steward, the bath steward, or the stewardess. If you are traveling tourist, 10 per cent of your passage cost is considered an adequate amount for tips. If you are traveling more luxuriously, in first or cabin classes, you are expected to pay a somewhat higher proportion for the service received.

After all is said about the amount of tips, it is well to remember that the manner in which the tip is given is fully as important as the tip itself. Waiters, bellboys, and manicurists are human beings and appreciate a smile and a "Thank you" just as anyone else does. Courtesy to them is fully as important as courtesy to any other group of people. And when you are on the receiving end of a tip, as thousands of college boys and girls are during summer work at resorts, for example, it is well to remember that the quality of the service and the spirit with which it is rendered have a definite relationship to the size of the tip and the spirit with which it is given.

Chapter Ten

PERSONAL APPEARANCE

WHAT WOULD YOU WEAR IF YOU WERE A MAN—IF YOU WERE A WOMAN *for a spring formal? for a Valentine tea dance at your favorite sorority house? for a formal evening reception for the President of the University given at the student-union building? for a luncheon given in a private home in honor of a visiting celebrity? for dinner the first night on shipboard? for a business interview with a prospective employer?*

WOULD YOU *ask your host or hostess what to wear for a certain occasion if you had no way of knowing whether formal or informal clothes were expected? wear your fraternity pin, athletic honor awards, or Phi Beta Kappa key when applying for a job? smoke in an employer's office? wear a maroon tie with your tuxedo?*

FROM EVERY SIDE we are bombarded by advertisers stressing the importance of making the best appearance possible. We are admonished that our hair, teeth, nails, and skin must be meticulously cared for, or we shall fail to be acceptable to the right person or organization and shall be overlooked for advancement in our jobs. We are told that unless our clothes are made by So-and-So and cleaned and pressed by Such-and-Such, success cannot be ours. We are fairly driven to the conclusion that the paint manufacturer who invented the slogan "Save the surface and you save all" was right.

It cannot be denied that appearance does count, for the man as well as for the woman. Many people with brains and with ability fail to achieve their maximum usefulness because they neglect their appearance. It is not the purpose of this chapter to present the point of view that success may be achieved by choosing the proper-colored necktie; but when medical schools are reported to be refusing admission to applicants whose trousers are not pressed, and employers deny girls jobs because they apply with their nails looking like "nothing human," it would appear that the subject of personal appearance deserves some attention. Brains are still more important than lipstick, and integrity more fundamental than haircuts, but a well-groomed appearance complements both brains and integrity.

A large group of employers, when asked to name the qualities that they wanted in the young people whom they employed, listed as being most important: honesty, judgment, initiative, industriousness, cooperativeness, and appearance. A good appearance is important because it is a factor in maintaining a good opinion of oneself, because it assists one to feel at ease in social situations, and because other people's reactions to one are affected by it.

One of the chief elements of personal appearance is one's posture. Drooping shoulders, a sunken chest, and protruding abdomen ruin the fit of the best suit or dress. Individual posture pictures, which can be obtained for a few cents in almost any well-equipped department of physical education, are valuable in showing up the items that need correction.

Even with all the modern aids to attractiveness, good health still remains the basis on which an attractive appearance is built. Cleanliness, neatness, and attention to details are today, as they were a hundred years ago, the indispensables of good grooming.

The Selection of Clothing

William James, the famous psychologist, wrote years ago that a youth transferred to the society of his betters could hardly ever learn to dress like a gentleman born. He said, "The merchants offer their wares as eagerly to him as to the veriest 'swell,' but he simply *cannot* buy the right things. An invisible law, as strong as gravitation, keeps him within his orbit, arrayed this year as he was the last; and how his better-bred acquaintances contrive to get the things they wear will be for him a mystery till his dying day."

Were William James alive today, he would no doubt concede that much of the mystery has been removed. Such magazines as *Vogue, Harper's Bazaar, Esquire, Mademoiselle, Charm,* and *Glamour,* as well as the so-called women's magazines and the fashion columns and advertisements in newspapers and magazines, tell us by illustrations as well as by words what is being worn. It is no longer necessary to have a queen's purse in order to purchase clothing of good design. Copies of the original models of French and American designers and of the tailoring of London's Bond Street soon appear in inexpensive models.

Fashion changes so rapidly that it is impossible to discuss here its current vagaries, but certain principles regarding the type of clothing suitable for wear on specific occasions can be touched upon. As all of us know, wearing the right kind of clothes for the occasion is an important factor in making us feel at ease in a social situation. A man who appears in a tuxedo when all the other men are in business suits, or a woman who wears a short dress when the other women guests are in long dresses, must be fairly experienced persons not to be uncomfortable in the situation and wish that he, or she, had stayed at home. The following suggestions are designed to help you choose the right clothes for various occasions.

FORMAL ATTIRE FOR WOMEN

"Of what does formal evening attire for women consist?"

Formal dress for a member of the younger crowd encompasses a greater variety of styles today than it did even a few years ago. The total effect aspired to is one of gaiety. Drabness is out. Color and sparkle are the order of the evening. Extreme hairdress and vivid nail polish and lipstick which would be out of place at noon are entirely acceptable at formal evening affairs.

The formal dress itself may be either a long formal, which is ankle length, or the currently more popular short formal or ballerina-length dress. It may have sleeves, but most often is sleeveless, if not, indeed, minus even shoulder straps themselves, but held in place by stiff bones sewed into the bodice. The variety of styling is equaled only by the variety of fabrics now considered appropriate for formal wear. All of the newer synthetic fabrics such as nylon, orlon, acetate, dacron, and vicara vie with such time-honored natural fabrics as silk and cotton. Prints, solid colors, pastels, and strong primary hues may be chosen as suits your fancy. It is difficult to characterize a formal dress specifically because, currently, scoop neckline, off-the-shoulder style, backless, sleeveless, and so on might describe a simple cotton sun dress as well as some formal evening dresses. In fact, many summer dresses especially do double duty.

On the other hand, there are formal dresses of ankle length, made of yards of billowing tulle or gossamer weave cotton that are formal wear and formal wear only. The variety acceptable is so great that your personal taste must and should be exercised. Evening slippers are of delicate fabric and construction and may be either pumps or sandals with high or low heels. Stockings are more sheer than those used for daytime wear. The evening bag is more delicate and dressy and of different style from the usual handbag. Jewelry may be worn as a complement to the costume, as may a corsage, but neither is necessary. Hats are usually not worn in the evening. The head may be covered by a scarf or by a small cap or hood if these are in fashion.

Few college women now have a coat that they use only for evening or formal wear. A "shortie" coat or a long one in white or pastel (washable, so that it will always be soft and spotless) is popular. Fur coats or jackets that do daytime duty are also acceptable for night formal wear.

A brief jacket, shrug, or stole can often convert a short formal into an acceptable afternoon tea or dinner dress, but this again will depend upon the type of formal dress you have chosen in the first place. If you want the dress to do double duty, you will select one with that in mind and forego the clouds of gossamer suitable only for formal wear.

The currently popular "shortie" glove coming only to the wrist can be purchased in white, a pastel shade, or any color you choose to complement your costume. White is always good.

Long gloves are not worn so much as formerly but are still in good taste. They are worn for dancing only at extremely formal affairs. They should either be worn in their entirety or removed; it is not in good taste to tuck the hand part under at the wrist.

Fraternity jewelry of any kind is "out" for formal wear. To wear a pin at a formal function marks you as not being in the know. Wrist watches, convenient though they would be, are not worn with formal dress unless they are very small, thin, or jeweled.

FORMAL ATTIRE FOR MEN

"What is considered correct formal attire for men?"

A black or midnight-blue dinner jacket or "tux" worn with matching trousers is acceptable formal attire or "evening clothes" for any formal evening occasion. You can wear this combination summer and winter, but in summer a lightweight white dinner jacket is more comfortable and to be preferred. A waistcoat is not a necessity, nor is a cummerbund, but the cummerbund is popular with college men. This will be black or blue silk to go with your dark dinner jacket or may be maroon with your summer white. Plaids and checks are available, but you may want to see how popular they are on your campus before you invest too heavily in them.

Your shirt must be white, but otherwise you can choose the style. The tie will be a black or blue bow, or, at most, maroon with your summer white, if you would stay on the conservative side. Your shoes must be black. Fashion dictates patent leather, but many college men make a plain black leather shoe with a leather sole (for dancing) serve their purpose. The socks are lightweight black or blue to match the trousers. Very few college men wear hats at all, but a black or blue Homburg for winter or fine Panama or Milan for summer is correct if you are inclined to wear one. Gray mocha, buck, or chamois gloves are part of the winter costume. Young men usually wear their everyday topcoats with their tuxedos. If the topcoat is to serve this purpose, it should be conservative in style and material. Loud plaid coats belong only in the wardrobe of the young man who has several coats from which to choose. A white linen handkerchief in your breast pocket and a red or white carnation in your lapel will complete your formal attire.

WHEN FORMAL DRESS IS WORN

"How do we know when to wear full evening dress?"

The form of the invitation usually will dictate what sort of dress you are to wear. Sometimes the word "formal" will be printed or engraved on the invitation. If the invitation is issued personally or by telephone, the host or hostess should state the type of dress expected. If you are uncertain, it is always better to ask than to be unhappy after you arrive because you are out of step with the others present.

"Do boys consider it poor taste for girls to ask whether or not they should wear formals to a spring party?"

No; it is correct to ask if the invitation does not state, and the host should be able to answer specifically and accurately.

"When an invitation to a 'pay' dance states on the tickets 'formal or informal,' what should guide one in the selection of formal or informal attire, provided you know no one else who is attending?"

You would be equally correctly dressed in either type of clothes. The important thing is for both the boy and the girl to wear the same kind. If the girl is wearing a "double duty" dress, not strictly formal, a ballerina-length one, for instance, with a jacket, shrug, or stole, the boy might wear his business suit or his tuxedo. If she wears a strictly formal dress, the boy will wear nothing less formal than his tuxedo. He should be guided by the girl's choice of clothes.

DRESS FOR INFORMAL SOCIAL OCCASIONS

Informal dances vary from those in which everyone goes in school clothes, to tea dances at which the guests are dressed in their best for daytime wear.

Unless the dance is definitely announced as a sports dance, which indicates, perhaps, the least formal variety, men are expected to wear coats and ties and girls street dresses. At sports dances, men wear slacks and sports coats; and girls, sweaters and skirts or other sports outfits. Accessories are in keeping with the costume chosen. Girls wear dressy shoes of leather or fabric to mixers and other informal affairs; men wear dark oxfords. At sports affairs, sport shoes are in order, provided the soles will permit dancing.

The important thing to remember is that accessories match the type of costume chosen. The answer to the question "Is it proper to wear a street dress and gold or silver evening sandals to an informal dance?" is "No." Formal accessories are out of place with informal clothes.

Women generally wear hats at tea dances in hotels or clubhouses. For luncheon, they wear dresses or suits in a great variety of fabrics, hats, and gloves and carry handbags. Hats are worn during the luncheon, whether it is in a hotel or in a private house. At a small, intimate luncheon, the hostess might, of course, ask her guests to remove their hats.

Adult visitors to the campus dress for the various social functions as they normally would for their own social functions back home in their own community. On the other hand the college community has its own accepted patterns for its own members. Thus, at a Mother's Day Luncheon or similar event, every mother in the room would probably be wearing her new spring hat and gloves, and carrying her prettiest handbag. Her daughter at her side would be hatless, gloveless, and bagless, but she would make a point of being meticulously groomed in a simple campus dress or suit with "hose and heels."

Her son, on her other side, might be wearing his best business suit or he might be wearing slacks and sports jacket, but he would have on a coat and tie in any case. "Coats on" for men is a "must" in practically any dining room, for any meal in any weather, except if there are directions from the hostess to the contrary or general group agreement to the contrary. The same rule holds for any evening social or official meeting that is not strictly stag and where you do not know of agreement to the contrary—whether it be on campus or off. You would never feel inappropriately dressed in a coat and tie for any ordinary social gathering.

AFTERNOON TEAS AND RECEPTIONS

"What is correct attire for an afternoon tea?"

At afternoon teas and receptions, men and women both wear the same kind of dress specified for luncheons. Women wear their hats and gloves. It is entirely permissible to shake hands with the hostess with gloves on. Gloves are usually worn until refreshments are served, when both gloves are removed. Hostesses often wear ballerina-length or so-called cocktail-length dresses and sometimes request those assisting them to do so. Assistants, if they are staying for some time, do not wear gloves, since they are hostesses in a sense. Guests who pour wear their hats. Even if a college girl is dropping in at a tea for only a moment, she should not wear her working costume of sweater and skirt and anklets, unless she knows that it is "that kind" of tea.

For dinner with any student group, such as a fraternity, sorority, cooperative house, or residence hall, simple street clothes are worn by the girls, and suits or jackets and slacks by the men. Hats are not worn for dinner. The "must" that will distinguish any kind of dress-up costume for girls from school clothes is "hose and heels" and for men it is "coat and tie." It is no compliment to the host or hostess, in the eyes of other diners, for either a girl or a boy to go to dinner at the other's place of residence on a spur-of-the-moment invitation unless he or she is presentably dressed for the occasion.

THEATER, OPERA, CONCERTS, CHURCH

Dress for the theater, opera, or concerts for the great majority of us in ninety-nine point nine per cent of the cases is street-length dress or business suit. In the evening women would take gloves and bag but probably wouldn't wear a hat because it would be a nuisance during the performance. This holds for the 44th Street Theater or the college auditorium. However, for anyone who is inclined to put on his best bib and tucker at the drop of a hat, these occasions offer an opportunity. Formal dress may be worn on any night if you are sitting in the orchestra (main floor) but would probably seem out of place in the balcony or gallery. More people dress formally on first nights or when a renowned artist is appearing than at other times. On the campus only the most careless of students would appear

at a university-sponsored function of this sort without coat and
tie or hose and heels.

In church, even more than in other public places, one should
avoid being conspicuous in dress. Women always wear hats and
keep them on during the service. Gloves also are worn but are
removed for communion. Women may shake hands with the
minister with their gloved hands. Men wear conservative suits,
shirts, ties, and socks.

CAMPUS WEAR

Most modern college campuses are laws unto themselves,
sartorially speaking. Campuses located downtown in a city feel
the restraining influence of the comparatively conservative business world near at hand, but those campuses outside the sphere
of influence—those schools located in small college towns from
one end of the country to the other—certainly make their own
laws of apparel.

In general, you can be certain that on almost any campus you
will encounter within the space of twenty-four hours on a week
end the complete range of attire from the most casual to the
most formal. The boy who lounges in the college sweet shop
over his belated morning coffee in the dirtiest of cords and most
disreputable lumberjack shirt open at the neck will ring the
doorbell of his favorite sorority house twelve hours later attired
in impeccable tux. The girl who has searched four solid hours
in a chem lab for an unknown, has spent two hours in lectures
and two more in committee meetings, dressed comfortably and
efficiently in sweater, skirt, ankle socks, and saddle shoes or
loafers, will appear in the reception room to greet her date of
the evening wearing the original of "that Ayres look" for the
debutante going to a party. "Appropriate to the deed thereof"
is happily the basic consideration for choice of clothes on the
campus, as elsewhere.

Without minimizing the importance of the current fads,

whether they be hand-decorated sweat shirts, plaid ear muffs, scarves, or knee-length knitted socks, for spicing your wardrobe, it may be said that there are certain costumes that serve virtually as the working uniform for the undergraduate. A man can be appropriately dressed for class or laboratory day in and day out in slacks, sport shirt, jacket, and sport shoes, and a girl, in sweater, skirt, ankle socks, and saddle shoes or loafers. The articles themselves are simple and unpretentious—distinction is achieved through expert choice of materials, colors, and pleasing combinations, plus good grooming. The colors, lines, and materials must be suited to your build and express in a certain sense your individual tastes. A judicious use of all of the common techniques of good grooming will enhance every good quality of the clothes themselves. You may discover the more subtle principles of the relation between design and individual body structure if you will discuss the matter with the home economics clothing expert of your school or with an intelligent buyer of men's or women's clothing for a good shop.

As for the importance of grooming, no imported fabric will take the place of a daily bath, nor will any pleasing line or color offset body odor or halitosis. A tweed jacket by Finchley profits a man nothing if his fingernails are dirty or he needs a haircut, any more than a Saks Fifth Avenue sports costume will profit a girl whose hair needs to be shampooed.

The "college uniform" can and should be varied frequently for the sake of the people who see one every day as well as for one's own social morale. Simple tailored suits or dresses in wool or practically any fabric worn with street shoes may alternate to advantage with the skirt-sweater-oxford or loafer combination, while an occasional business suit, with coat and trousers matching, and with a plain shirt and tie are certainly not amiss. The temptation is sometimes strong to wear cast-off best dresses for school; but to the question "Is a taffeta dress 'out' for campus wear?" the answer must be a definite "Yes, completely out," if you would look appropriately dressed for your work. If you can't change the whole costume, try varying the accessories to give yourself a mental lift.

The matter of shoes never seems to cause men half the difficulty that it causes women. At least men's heels are always low, and they don't have to decide how high they can wear them and still get around. On most campuses, there is so much walking to be done that comfortable walking shoes have come into their own for both men and women. It might be said, however, that a boy needs at least one pair of very dark cordovan brown oxfords for his more conservative moods and a pair of plain black shoes to go with his tux. The usual combination oxfords in black and white or brown and white, or heavy gum-soled moccasins, do not go well with your best dark suit for informal dances or for church. Nor, on the other hand, can any girl afford to become so fond of her comfort that she detracts from the attractive appearance of her best tailored suit or dress by putting on a pair of misshapen ballet shoes with it. The question

"Is it proper to wear high heels to classes? What about spectator pumps?"

can certainly be answered in the affirmative if the wearer will use common sense as to how high "high" may mean. High French, or spike, heels are definitely out of place on the campus, because they neither fit in with the kind of clothes one wears nor are practical for walking. Spectator pumps or any so-called street shoes with walking heels are appropriate and often complement a tailored costume far better than the beloved flats.

"Should white shoes be worn all winter?"

would certainly be answered in the negative, if only the principles of art in costume were considered. To attract attention to the feet is seldom desirable, but it is obvious that this is accomplished by combining white shoes with dark winter clothing.

On the other hand, one of the fads of the moment on many campuses is soiled white shoes with anything. Interestingly enough this fad is followed perhaps more by men students bent on being collegiate than by women, although some women, too, are moved by this fashion of the moment.

Another fad of the moment among women is the wearing of ballet-type shoes that have little to recommend them. They can't be called flattering since they give almost all wearers the look of thick ankles and knobby muscles; nor are they good for the feet since they give no support. Like the soiled white shoes they are "good" only because the campus says so, not because they carry the fashion experts' approval.

HATS AND GLOVES

Many college men and women aren't bothered by the problem of what hats or gloves to wear on the campus—they just don't wear any. Of course, a really cold morning brings out a variety of headcoverings both among men and women students. Bright-colored ear muffs appear on otherwise unprotected heads both masculine and feminine. Jackets with hoods or parkas attached are popular with both sexes. Some boys unearth their hunting caps with ear flaps and others wear tight-fitting knit wool caps. The girls wrap up their heads in colorful wool stoles with the ends crisscrossed and flung jauntily back over their shoulders. Whenever gloves appear, they are warm and preferably gay and colorful, whether of the knitted wool or leather variety.

SPORTS CLOTHES

The term sports clothes refers currently to many informal dresses or casual separates as well as to those which are designed for particular sports. Let it be said to the credit of designers and manufacturers that good-looking, beautifully tailored costumes for every variety of activity are plentiful. The two-piece slack suit for men, in pleasing solid colors or in the gayest of prints, is bringing a colorful note and summer comfort to men's attire. Well-cut slacks, shorts, culottes, play suits, and so on are encouraging girls to look trim and appropriately dressed for hikes, picnics, and games. The problem now of looking well in active sports clothes is one of becoming selection and the same attention to grooming that is necessary when one dresses for the street. Both young men and women know that it takes real attention to detail to achieve a casual look and that casual is far from synonymous with sloppy.

Every sport from horseback riding to hockey has its distinctive costume. Although it isn't necessary to have a complete and separate costume for everything that you may attempt, it is important to have clothing that will permit you the physical freedom that the activity itself requires and will give you the self-confidence that comes from knowing that you are appropriately dressed. There is the further point that some games or sports require certain personal equipment from the player as a protection to the grounds or equipment of the sport itself. The leather heels of ordinary oxfords will cut up a clay tennis court, and the high heel of a woman's street shoe will make damaging holes in a golf green. A distinguishing mark of a sportsman is his appreciation of equipment as well as the quality of his sportsmanship.

Current fashion magazines, newspaper advertisements, or a trip to the sportswear section of a good clothing or department store will bring you up to date on what is being worn for tennis, golf, skiing, skating, swimming, or sun bathing.

Probably the most important things to remember when you are getting ready for any sport are, first, that the costume should be one in which you will be comfortable doing the particular activity of your choice, and, second, that the different items of a sports costume must belong together as truly as do those of your best street ensemble. High-heeled slippers do not go with slacks any more than saddle oxfords go with a navy blue silk travel suit. An impeccable white piqué tennis dress won't necessarily make you a champion any more than a set of Ben Hogan irons will make you a golfer, but it will help your game and boost your morale when you begin to think that you never can learn that backhand!

DRESS FOR THE BUSINESS INTERVIEW

Clothing for business itself, or for the business of getting a job, is a different matter from clothing for campus or sportswear. On campuses, it has somehow become established that one may dress casually; but, on the whole, the business world is still to be convinced of the desirability of casual clothes. For business, you have to look as if you meant business. Lyons and Martin, in *The Strategy of Job Finding*, urge young men and women who are looking for jobs to remember that literally hundreds of personnel managers have stated that inappropriate dress is one of the chief handicaps of the average college man or woman. In their opinion, the young man who appears for a business interview in sports clothes, with droopy socks and sans hat, or the young woman who appears in an afternoon dress or without stockings when she is applying for a job has handicapped himself or herself unduly.

It is well known that some businesses specify the type of clothing that their employees may wear while others resort to uniforms in order to achieve the simplicity that the firms desire. When you spend time and money to fit yourself for a job, you ought consciously to put your best foot forward to get it. Your first consideration is to look as if you fitted better than anyone else the position for which you are applying. Your general appearance, what you look like as a whole, will be the impression that the interviewer will gather first. Therefore, before you set forth, whether you be man or woman, ask someone whose opinion you value to look you over and pass judgment. Details or total effects are sometimes more discernible to another than to yourself. A full-length mirror, though not an equivalent, is recommended as a substitute for friendly criticism. Your attractiveness during a job interview as at any other time is a combination of clothing and grooming.

Everyone has some personal choice in the selection of his or her clothes but no choice in whether he or she will be well groomed. You must be clean, your hair must have been recently shampooed and be neat in appearance, your nails must be clean and of inconspicuous length, you must be free of body odor and bad breath, shoes well kept and clothes well pressed.

FOR WOMEN

If your clothes are of good design and well made, and if you wear them with ease and grace, you will be attractive. A touch of your most becoming color in your handkerchief, necklace, collar, or belt will be a pleasing note. Some interesting detail at the neckline of your suit or dress will help make your face, and its expression, the point of emphasis. Authorities warn frankly against too low-cut necklines and not wearing girdles, brassières, and slips, even in the summer. It is obvious that no employer is going to bother to admit you to his organization and try to correct such omissions later. Be sure that your skirt is long enough and full enough that you can sit on any office chair with dignity, confident that not too great a length of stocking is exposed.

A favorite technique of employers to discover just how neat you are is to ask you to remove your hat or perhaps your coat. Your hair arrangement should be neat and becoming enough to stand such inspection, and your coat lining will have to be mended and clean to pass the test. Never doubt that a keen interviewer will see the contents of your purse if you open it, and he may believe that there is a definite relation between its neatness and that of your desk or file.

Each of your accessories, from your hat to your shoes, will be appraised by a trained eye. A small hat designed so that some of your face and hair are visible gives the interviewer a chance to see *you*; immaculate gloves and bag in harmony with your costume; street shoes, appropriate for the work that you will be doing; and a spotlessly fresh handkerchief will help make you look more poised than perhaps you feel. To wear ornate jewelry, a veil that covers your face, too much perfume, and chipped nail polish is tempting fate in most cases. Fraternity and sorority pins are out of place in a business interview. Some employers feel keenly on this point, and you can't afford not to pay attention to the point of view of the person who has the job to fill.

Something borrowed may be indispensable for your wedding but dangerous for an interview. You need to feel at home. An actual instance recently brought to our attention illustrates this point. An attractive young secretary who had a scholarship in a well-known secretarial school was recommended to a desirable employer. The school told him what a good record she had made all through college despite her having to earn much of her expenses. In her efforts to make a good appearance, she borrowed everything from a mink coat to a velvet toque. The result was that she was distinctly out of character in relation to the person that he expected to see, and he didn't offer her the job.

FOR MEN

Men as well as women have to guard against loud or conspicuous clothes if they would do themselves justice. It is probably better that your suit material should be so conservative in pattern that the interviewer will wonder afterward exactly what it was than that he should wonder why you ever thought that

that coat and pair of trousers could be worn together. Frayed cuffs, soiled collars, unshined shoes, unpressed trousers, and crumpled handkerchiefs are much more apt to harden an employer's heart against you than to melt it in your favor.

On the other hand, a clean-shaven face, immaculate hands and nails, and well-brushed hair, which is neither shaggy nor shorn for the occasion, will go a long way toward getting you a chance to show what you can do. Experts in personnel warn men against eye-catching belt buckles; pens and pencils worn in the outside coat pocket; miniature footballs, baseballs, and similar decorations dangling too conspicuously from watch chains; and ornate rings or pins displayed injudiciously. A Phi Beta Kappa key is considered all right for men but not for women.

Men and women both should remember that cigarette-stained fingers and teeth may mean to an employer that the applicant can't get along without his hourly cigarette. Entering an office with a lighted cigarette or smoking without being invited to do so may offend an employer out of all proportion to the importance of the act itself. Unfortunately, all too many boys and girls don't appreciate how keenly some employers feel about an applicant's chewing gum or "wearing" a toothpick! "Oral failings," in the same class with halitosis, these habits have been aptly called! And remember that you are the guest in a host's office for the time being and you may not partake of his hospitality even to the extent of sitting down until you have been invited to do so.

In brief, it might be said that the success of a business interview is usually so important to the future of the young man or woman concerned that then, if ever, is the time to exercise all one's techniques for pleasing the other person, regardless of whether wearing the right clothes or doing the right thing seems important in and of itself. It's a plain paying matter.

Dress for Travel, Week-end Visits, and Conferences

Trips, week-end visits, and conferences force us to organize our wardrobes more carefully than we ever have to while we stay at home where we have our complete resources at hand. The desirability of owning one set of accessories, including hat, bag, gloves, and shoes, that will harmonize with more than one dress or suit is borne in upon us as we pack our traveling bags.

The truth is that a little careful planning of a total wardrobe will pay dividends day in and day out, as well as for special trips. Everyone admires the man or woman who always looks "put together." In all probability, it is no accident that John Jones's overcoat, hat, and gloves go well both with his new brown suit and with his last fall's green tweed or that Mary Smith doesn't have to buy a different spring hat to go with her new tailored suit. They both no doubt gave a little thought to the types of clothes that they would need for different occasions and selected items that would fit into various combinations, some of which, at least, they already owned. Trips, visits, and conferences present no needs particularly different from everyday needs, but they do demand that we check our wardrobes against our program of activities in order that the appropriate costume may be assembled at the proper time.

Week-end invitations that specify that there will be a golf game Saturday afternoon and an informal dance at the country club Saturday night and church with the family Sunday morning are more helpful than invitations that leave the guest wondering what activities he should provide for.

For traveling by train or plane, many women feel better turned out in dark, tailored street clothes and prefer to introduce their favorite color notes through blouses and accessories, but the advent of the synthetic washable miracle fabrics has made light-colored travel clothes increasingly popular. Most men, too, dress for the street rather than in sports things when they travel by public conveyance, although one has only to watch the passengers alighting from a transcontinental plane at any of the big airports to see that more and more men are dressing for comfort when they travel. If one is traveling by car, he will, of course, be governed by the sort of things that he plans to do en route. Camping out overnight along the way obviously calls for different clothes from those required by overnight stops at a downtown hotel.

Daytime shipboard life finds passengers attired in comfortable casual sports wear suitable for lounging or active deck sports. However, nearly everyone will change into something fresh and less casual for dinner. Dinner aboard ship is always informal the first night out, regardless of the class of passage. After the first night, dress is optional. Formal attire for dinner will be indicated in some manner if it is expected.

For any trip, an experienced traveler will take at least one pair of comfortable walking shoes for sightseeing, a lightweight warm coat which can withstand evening breezes, and a lightweight raincoat that he hopes may be left rolled up in his suitcase. For most extensive trips it is also advisable to take dinner clothes. You are almost certain to need them at some time.

Chapter Eleven

ENGAGEMENTS AND WEDDINGS

THERE IS PROBABLY no subject more in the minds and hearts of most young people than that of their own marriage. Not necessarily that they talk most about it, nor admit the personal importance of the subject to their parents, their friends, or themselves; many of them don't! Underneath the restless urge toward social activity with the opposite sex, however, is the conviction on the part of a great many boys and girls that it is all-important, eventually, to find the person one can share all sorts of experiences with happily. While the sociologists would no doubt account for the present lower average marriage age by dozens of contributing factors, it is important from the point of view of this book not so much to explain why young men and women are marrying at an earlier age than did their parents, but to recognize that this is so. Young men and women—students in colleges and high schools or workers in business and industry —are marrying in tremendous numbers and at a relatively early age.

This fact accounts, no doubt, for the hundreds of questions regarding engagements and weddings that are asked by young people in the more recent survey that did not appear at all in the earlier survey. It also probably accounts for the wide treatment of the subject in current books on social usage and in current magazines. As in many other areas of social usage, the writers have recognized that many questions of procedure involving standard accepted practice are fully covered in other publications readily available. For that reason this chapter deals primarily with the problems that confront young people who are trying to manage a wedding themselves in addition to a job—whether the job be that of paid employee or student—or are participating in the activities of their young friends who are being married. Practically every illustration drawn or example cited based on the customs of student living groups applies equally to young people in a working situation.

It was not so very many years ago that a married student, man or woman, among the undergraduate students of any of our colleges or universities was a rarity. The occasional girl who eloped with her fiancé in January instead of waiting for a proper June wedding caused great consternation both to college authorities and her parents. That the married couple should settle down a week later in a university-sponsored housing development for married students and finish their college work together was practically undreamed of. Happily, elopements are even scarcer today than formerly. Happily, also, there are married students by the hundreds on our campuses. During the past few years we have seen many women students finishing their college work while their husbands were away in military service.

On the other hand, hundreds of college men, after completing their military service, returned to their college campus to complete their formal education. Many of these combined an academic education with the first years of married life, alternating hours of classroom lectures with periods of family shopping or minding junior. Likely as not, the wife worked seven or eight hours a day in some professor's office or laboratory to supplement the G.I. subsistence check. And in the most recent years we have moved into an era in which many young men and women have been intent upon crowding as much of life and living as they can into the few years prior to military service. In a good many cases this has meant marriage and continuing school together.

Without any attempt at evaluating this phenomenon of the current social scene sociologically, it must be recognized as an aspect of modern life of tremendous interest and importance to young people of eighteen and nineteen to twenty-two and twenty-three. Students, both women and men, from one end of the country to the other ask:

"*Is it advisable for a girl to become engaged during her college career?*"

"*At what age is marriage advisable for a man in our present economic system?*"

"*How long should a couple go together before marriage?*"

"*Do you think that it is right for young people who have met in college to marry and continue school together?*"

"*Is it wise to continue school after you are married?*"

"*Have the marriages of college students been found to be as successful as regular ones?*"

Whether the marriage of college students is advisable or wise or right is beyond the scope of this particular book, but, fortunately, many of our high schools, colleges, and universities have recognized the need of young people to formulate patterns of action in these areas. Credit courses in "Marriage and Family Life" are increasingly available. Counselors trained in the art and techniques of helping young people think through their own particular situation and make constructive decisions can be found under one title or another in practically any school situation and in some business organizations. If this whole matter is very much on your mind, seek out the adult in your environment whom you feel you can talk with. It may be your dean of boys or girls, your dean of men or women, or your personnel director. It may be your physical-education teacher or your home-economics teacher. It may be your pastor, your school or company nurse, or the doctor at the health service or a young married couple who has met personally the problem which you would like to discuss.

The important thing is to realize that lots of other young people are puzzled in regard to this whole area and that, for the most part, adults who work with young people in one way or another these days recognize your problems, too, and are ready to help you work them out. There is evidence available in the files of any college today that some married students have established *excellent* academic records. Married students themselves will testify that you can be married, you can continue in school, and you can make a success of both—but it takes a lot of doing. They warn you not to underestimate the problems of adjustment to married life—"It's a lot different being married to a fellow when you sit down to three meals a day *by yourselves* than it is just going out on dates and parties with lots of other people." "You think things are going to go along just the same as they have been, but you suddenly find that both of you have sides you never knew about. Your family has always done things one way and her family has always done them another. You have to work out your own way together—and sometimes that's hard—but it's fun."

Whether it is advisable or wise or right for you to become engaged or married at any particular point in your life is something that only the two of you can finally decide. If the decision is made in harmony with your parents, and after careful consideration of all of the pros and cons, the chances that it will be a wise one are certainly increased. In any case, the decision regarding marriage is probably the most important one that any individual ever makes in so far as his or her own personal happiness is concerned. From this fact follows the clear implication that every ounce of your intelligence, your emotional maturity, your understanding must be brought to bear upon the decision.

"GOING STEADY"

So the two of you are "going steady" or are "pinned." Are you engaged? The interpretation of "going steady" or being "pinned" varies so much from campus to campus, and even from individual to individual, that you owe it to yourselves and your friends to clarify your relationship. This is just good sense as far as the two of you are concerned. You certainly don't want any misunderstanding between you as to whether this is merely a convenient dating arrangement or whether this represents the serious choice of both of you as to your future plans for marriage, home, and family. Your parents, friends, and community need to know, too, otherwise they don't really know how the relationship should be treated. You can afford to be vague about some things, but this calls for clear definition.

The only way to answer your questions, "What is the difference between 'pinning' and 'engagement'" or "What is the difference between 'going steady' and 'being engaged'" is to emphasize that "pinning" and "going steady" can and do mean different things to different people, and that, if you are doing either one, you had better define for yourselves and friends exactly what *you* mean by it. On the other hand, "being engaged" means clearly that the two of you plan to be married, are so committed to each other, and should be so considered by anyone else interested.

The engagement period obviously presents new problems for decision to both the man and the woman. Worded one way or another, one of the most troublesome questions seems to be whether it's "right," "proper," "improper," "all right," "good taste," "permissible," for either one of the couple to date anyone else if the other member of the team is not in the same town and, therefore, not available to share social events. And again, the only answer possible is that the two of you together must decide what is wise and best for you. The answer will not be the same for every couple. There are pros and cons, advantages and hazards, either way.

The important thing would seem to be complete understanding and mutual agreement as to the course of action to be followed. Too much cannot be said for frankness of discussion and understanding of each other's point of view in this matter. Certainly no man or woman wants to fly under false colors under any circumstances.

If you do decide to participate in the social life around you, when the one you'd like most to be dating is far, far away, then by all means make it clear to the boy or girl who makes it possible for you to participate, exactly what your status is. No taking off the engagement ring and leaving it in the bureau drawer for your own convenience! No kissing the girl good-night and making her think you think she is the answer to your prayer when she really isn't! On the other hand, participation in group social functions or informal visiting over a cup of coffee or a Coke with another man or woman is not going to jeopardize your engagement relationship.

Before a young person can answer a good many of the questions that come to mind about what is expected and acceptable behavior during the engagement period, he or she might try to define in his own mind, at least, just what purpose the engagement period can and should serve. It can serve many useful purposes. One of the most useful ones mentioned by young people themselves is that it should offer opportunities to get acquainted with each other's family and to see and understand the other person in his family relationships. If young people meet and become engaged when either one or both are away from home, it is quite likely that they have not had this opportunity too often before. But this is an important aspect of both the engagement and marriage relationship.

IN EACH OTHER'S HOME

A boy often looks different in his own home setting than he does glamorously turned out in a tux with a carnation in his lapel. And it's just as well to know whether a girl is good at assuming household responsibilities or whether she sits around while her mother waits on her hand and foot. As a matter of fact, some young people believe that it is much better to visit in each other's home before you decide to be engaged at all.

Fortunately, one of the happier customs of current campus life is going home for a week end once in a while with a friend, either boy or girl. It is acceptable in most circles either to issue or accept such an invitation if you make sure that arrangements have been cleared with the mother who will serve as hostess for the event. Time was when such plans called for a direct invitation to the boy or girl guest from the mother hostess, but arrangements made by either son or daughter directly, specifically approved by the mother, now seem to be sufficient. It is taken for granted that no girl will accept such an invitation from a boy or his family without full cognizance and approval of her own family.

To the question "Is it acceptable for an engaged couple to take a week-end trip if staying at a respectable place" the answer is still "no"—not by yourselves. Group trips with an older married couple or some older woman along on the party is still the expected and accepted pattern. A young woman does not go alone to a young man's apartment after dinnertime at night, even though engaged to him, if either she or the man values her reputation in such matters. Neither should she entertain the young man alone in her apartment if she would be entirely free of criticism. Joint enterprises including one or two other couples are still the order of the day, even if one has achieved an apartment of one's own.

"How intimate should an engaged couple become?" is a frank wording of a very real problem. Authorities in the marriage and family-life areas have tried to answer the question objectively. They recognize the human desire and need for a warm, close, affectionate relationship and urge that such be established, but still within limitations. Their clinical experience in dealing with many married couples seeking help leads them to advise against pre-marital sexual relationships. At the same time that they advise in favor of a long enough engagement period to allow time for becoming thoroughly acquainted and for making adequate plans for marriage they advise against a long period of two or three years as being full of frustrations and tensions.

No one can say whether a three months' engagement or a fifteen months' engagement is the perfect length of time. Again, only the couple themselves can answer their own question, but they should certainly try to answer in the light of known facts as well as on an emotional basis. As far as authorities in the field know, students who marry and remain in school are as likely to have successful marriages as those who marry under other circumstances. Indeed, there is some observable evidence to support the belief that students who marry happily while still in school may achieve better academic records after marriage than they did before when they spent too much time dating.

The engagement period does afford a period of time for carrying out all the traditional social customs connected with a wedding. The first step unquestionably is serious discussion by the two of you of the kind of wedding you want, for it can be as elaborate or as simple as you want it and still be in good taste. Many items will enter into your decision, and not the least of these should be a frank consideration of the cost involved in the various possible arrangements and how much you and your families can afford to spend. Consideration should also be given to the expenses involved for your friends whom you ask to participate in the wedding. You should do some detailed budget planning before you make a decision, if the money expended is going to be a matter of concern to you as it is to most people.

Weddings and the demand for goods and services in connection with them have come to be recognized as a focal point around which much productive advertising and good customer relations can be developed by department stores and specialty shops. When you consider everything, from the stationery for the invitations to the selection of a spot for the honeymoon, and then think of the silver, linen, china, glassware, flowers, home furnishings, special clothing, and dozens of other items you will become involved in, you can see why this would be true. A tremendous amount of advertising relative to these goods and services, along with detailed articles on every conceivable aspect of wedding planning, are to be found in several current publications devoted to the subject. Such quarterly publications as *The Bride's Magazine,* the *Modern Bride,* and *House Beautiful's Guide for the Bride* are available on practically every drugstore magazine rack. For fifty cents or a dollar, one of these will supply you with dozens of useful ideas in addition to accurate information, complete with diagrams, on various types of weddings, receiving lines for the reception, etc.

Most large department stores now have bridal consultants, home-planning consultants, gift consultants, and such special-service personnel on their staffs. A typical issue of *The Bride's Magazine,* for instance, lists some 250 stores in 117 different cities each of which has on its staff from one to four consultants in these areas. These people are experts on every detail of wedding cost and planning, and their services are free to you on the theory that you or the people who will give you gifts will make some of the wedding purchases at their store. If the two of you would spend an evening leafing through one of the publications mentioned and then spend an hour or so in conference with the bridal consultant of the store most convenient for you, you would have some pretty definite ideas of costs, variety of plans possible, and how you wanted to proceed from there.

One of the first things a bridal consultant will try to persuade you to do is to work out a time schedule of what is to be done, when, and by whom, in the light of the date you have chosen for your wedding. She will probably produce time-schedule forms reminiscent of your freshman study schedule but none the less useful if you wish to accomplish this undertaking in an orderly fashion. She may also present you with budget forms, check lists, and such booklets as *The Bride's Book of Plans, Esquire's Guide for the Bridegroom,* and a copy of the latest issue of *The Bride's Magazine.* The main point of all this discussion is to assure you that a great variety of service, advice, and counsel is free to you for the asking. Young married couples who have somehow managed weddings along with their school work or full-time jobs, urge you to make use of these services as the most practical approach to your wedding.

ANNOUNCING THE ENGAGEMENT

"When is it proper to announce one's engagement?"

"Does the mother at home or the daughter at school announce the engagement?"

"Should you wait to announce your engagement until you have a diamond?"

"Is it proper to send a printed engagement card?"

As soon as you two have decided to be engaged you must decide the answer to "When should the engagement be announced?" And the answer is certainly a matter of your preference. Once you tell anybody or announce it in any way it becomes official. The girl's parents send the information to the hometown newspaper. If you, as a bride-elect, plan to announce the engagement at a party for some of your friends, then the newspaper announcement can be marked for release so as not to spoil your surprise for your guests. You can manage this even if you are away at school just as long as you and your mother plan together on the timing of events. You don't have to have a diamond either to be engaged or to announce your engagement officially through the newspaper or in other ways. If your plans call for a long engagement period of two or three years, you can afford to give yourselves a longer time before you announce the engagement. Both of you will always have certain friends that you will want to tell the good news to personally or by a personal note once you two together have decided to tell anyone. Printed or engraved announcement cards are sometimes used, but they haven't yet achieved the acceptability of the handwritten note.

Every campus has its own customs about announcing the engagement to your college mates. There are the traditional pin-serenades staged by the fraternity or residence-hall group when one of its members gives his pin or ring seriously. This is followed by the correspondingly traditional way of responding to this particular kind of serenade on the part of the girls' living unit. They may sing a special response, or arrange themselves dramatically on the winding stairs, or hold candles at the windows while their engaged member goes out on the steps to receive the special attention of the visitors, or follow any other special ritual they may have worked out for such an occasion. In some places the traditional box of candy is sent by the man to the girl to share with her living group and cigars are passed by him to his housemates. You won't be around any campus or office very long without observing what its customs are, so you will be well prepared to fall in line when the time comes.

Invitations give the necessary information as to time and place of the wedding. Whether you use the formal engraved invitation with its set pattern of words or a handwritten informal one depends more upon the size of your wedding than on whether it is to be held at church or home or is considered formal or informal in terms of dress, number of attendants, time of day, etc. Some people choose to have a very small guest list. If this is your choice, handwritten invitations, on good quality plain white note paper, sent out by the bride's mother are perfectly acceptable. If there are to be many invitations issued, engraved ones are in order. There is still a feeling among oldsters that engraving, and engraving only, is acceptable for wedding invitations. Some of the younger generation, however, insist that there are now new processes, not printing and yet not engraving, that look and feel like engraving but are not nearly so expensive. At least it is your privilege to investigate thermography or similar processes and see whether it will meet your requirements. You will want to examine samples at the stationery counter of a department store or at the printing and engraving company. You will have a choice as to quality of paper stock and whether to use one or two envelopes, but the form will be the prescribed one and the paper will be a white double sheet with fold on left side.

Mr. and Mrs. William King
request the honor of your presence
at the marriage of their daughter
Mary
to
Mr. Raymond Charles Clark
on Friday, the ninth of June
one thousand nine hundred and fifty-four
at twelve o'clock
Saint Mary's Church
Libertyville, Ohio

It is well to order "informals" at the same time, for you will need appropriate white note paper for thank-you notes to acknowledge your gifts almost as soon as the invitations are mailed. The advice of those who have been through the experience is to acknowledge your shower gifts and wedding gifts as promptly as you humanly can if you would not let the task assume gigantic proportions. It's a time-worn custom that the bride becomes the family correspondent, but she makes a point of expressing the groom's pleasure in the gift received as well as her own. The thank-you note should (1) indicate that you know what the gift was, (2) the pleasure of both of you in the gift, and (3) some personal touch to individualize the note.

Dear Mrs. Wilson,

The silver tray that you and Mr. Wilson sent John and me is indeed handsome. We both love it and we'll enjoy using it. We hope that both of you will enjoy your trip to Florida next month. In March we expect to go to Chicago and hope we may have a visit with you then. Meanwhile, we thank you for the beautiful gift.

Sincerely yours,
Mary Brown

Your time schedule will tell you that each of you should start making your invitation lists as soon as you know what kind of wedding you are to have. Ask the engraver for the envelopes as soon as you place your invitation order so that you can start addressing them. The invitations should be in the mail three weeks before the wedding date. If you use the two-envelope arrangement, the outer envelope is addressed as an ordinary letter. The inner one carries the name only such as Mr. and Mrs. Jones, and is left unsealed.

If you are the recipient of a wedding invitation by itself, you do not have to reply to it except, of course, if it is one of the informal friendly handwritten ones. That kind does demand a reply in kind, promptly. If you are invited to the reception following the wedding, then you should reply so that reasonably accurate planning can be done by your hostess.

An engraved wedding invitation does not necessarily require a gift; you are free to send one or not as you choose. A handwritten personal invitation does, however, require a gift. It need not be elaborate, but you should manage something. A wedding announcement sent after the wedding does not require a gift or any acknowledgment, although a note in return is certainly in order. If you are invited to the reception, even if you cannot attend, you should still send a gift. The same response is expected to an invitation to a shower, whether or not you can attend it.

The weddings of several college classmates or of friends from your own house, dormitory, or office following each other in close succession can put a financial strain on you if you are one of the great majority of closely budgeted young people. Unless the person or persons being married are very, very close to you and you want to give a gift personally, a group gift to which you contribute will certainly serve the purpose. Many living units such as residence-hall corridor groups, sororities, fraternities, and cooperative houses, as well as office groups in a working situation, have a standing custom that they don't give individual gifts to their members, but that all members contribute a small amount to a group gift.

Wedding gifts may be sent at any time, but before the wedding they are always addressed to the bride and sent to her home. Afterward they are sent to the home of the newly married couple and addressed to both bride and groom. Since the bride often wishes to arrange a display of the gifts for all to see during the reception, it is well to send the gift a few days before the wedding. If, for any reason, plans for the wedding are canceled, the girl is expected to return wedding gifts to the senders with brief notes that the wedding will not take place. She may make an explanation if she wishes but certainly is not required to do so.

While traditionally every girl would probably prefer to be married in her own home town, if she is in college she is often faced with the fact that most of her friends, as well as those of her fiancé, are in school with her. If her home happens to be hundreds of miles away, then it becomes a choice between being married at home and being married at school where the friends can be a part of the wedding and its festivities. As a result of this dilemma, the student churches and church foundations around college campuses have been the scenes of many a student wedding, and the residence hall or sorority house the happy setting of the reception following the ceremony. When this kind of arrangement is decided upon, the girl must assume the responsibility for taking care of an infinite number of details that she would have her mother's help on if her wedding were to be at home. On the other hand, planning the home wedding mostly by correspondence and the occasional trip home that can be squeezed in on a week end is not easy either, as those who have done it will testify. In either case the answer seems to be systematic organization—lists concerning everybody and everything and a time schedule that provides for getting everything done by a specified time without fail. Luckily, as college students or paid employees, you are accustomed to tight schedules and deadlines; so this approach will not be too different a way of handling the project.

SIMPLE OR ELABORATE

As was mentioned previously, your wedding can be as simple or as elaborate in terms of setting and number of other people involved as you want it. Since this is true, it seems more important to emphasize the free advising and consulting service available to you through department- and specialty-store wedding consultants, and the materials they will give you, than to try to elaborate on all of the details of suitable clothes, proper seating, or accepted order of standing in a receiving line. Such information to meet your particular requirements for either the small or large wedding of your choice is readily available to you. You may certainly also do as you choose about having a reception. To the question "Is it always necessary to have a reception following a wedding?" the answer is "No." The two of you may choose to stand at the rear of the church or in the vestibule and accept the good wishes of your friends if you would rather do it that way.

Young people ask a great many questions that reflect their need to know how some of the financial aspects of a wedding are handled before they go too far with plans.

"*Is it permissible to ask the bridesmaids to buy their own gowns when the bride specifies the type?*"

"*Is there any rule of etiquette that says who should buy the bride's hope chest?*"

"*Should the groom pay for wedding pictures if the bride's family doesn't feel capable?*"

"*Should the man or his fiancée buy the man's wedding ring?*"

BRIDESMAIDS

The matter of bridesmaids does present problems. It is considered an honor to be invited to be a bridesmaid—and the bride intends her invitation to convey this feeling to her friends or relatives whom she invites to serve her. At the same time, it is customary for the bridesmaids to pay for their own dresses as selected by the bride to fit into her whole wedding pattern. This means that the bride needs to give special thought to the cost of the dresses she selects for her bridesmaids to wear. They should, if possible, be of a style and general type that a girl might find some use for later as a part of her wardrobe.

Corresponding things may be said for the best man and

ushers. The groom is showing his feeling of friendship for the men he invites to participate in his wedding. The men in turn are responsible for their own clothing and are expected to bear any expense necessary to outfit themselves as the wedding plans demand, except that identical boutonnières, ties, and gloves are supplied by the groom.

The bridesmaids are the guests of the bride, and the best man and ushers the guests of the groom as far as any living expenses are concerned after they arrive in the town in which the wedding is being held. They are all, men and women alike, responsible for their own transportation expenses to the town of the wedding.

The cedar chest or "hope chest" itself, as well as its contents of household and personal linens, are an expense of the bride and her family. Many linens, both household and personal, are accumulated, however, through the kindness and thoughtfulness of friends who give showers in honor of the bride.

PICTURES

Wedding pictures are a part of the pre-wedding expense and as such are the responsibility of the bride and her family. Some brides' parents operating sensibly on a budget meet this responsibility by specifying that they will pay a given amount toward picture expense. Thus, if the bride and groom together decide they want more pictures than the specified amount will provide, it becomes their responsibility to arrange with the photographers to bill them later for anything in excess of the specified allowance. In this way the groom can make his contribution.

The expenses connected with a wedding are divided according to a traditional pattern of long standing. The bride and her family are responsible for

Wedding invitations, reception invitations, and announcements

Organist, soloist, church janitor, or sexton

Bridesmaids' bouquets and presents for them

Bride's wedding dress, clothes, household linens, wedding pictures

Reception: food, flowers, transportation from church to the reception

The man's wedding ring if one is used

The groom is responsible for

Engagement ring

Wedding ring

Marriage license

Bride's bouquet and going-away corsage and flowers for both mothers to wear at the wedding

Best man's and ushers' identical boutonnières, ties, gloves, and presents

Monetary gift to minister, priest, or rabbi

Automobile to leave reception

Honeymoon

Here is a firsthand report on wedding arrangements from one of the popular happily married undergraduate women on a big Middle Western college campus. She was married during the Christmas holidays of her senior year when her Army-officer bridegroom could get a short leave—enough for the wedding and a brief honeymoon. When he returned to his West Coast station, she returned to her sorority house on campus and picked up the threads of a busy undergraduate life—senior in vocational home economics, president of Mortar Board, senior women's honorary, etc.

"Planning a formal wedding and large reception when the bride-to-be is attending college and the groom is in the Service is a challenge, but with a carefully organized time sched-

ule, and with lots of air-mail stamps, it can be done. The difficulties encountered are: having to do most of the planning by mail, and not being able to enjoy the mother-daughter enthusiasm of the out-of-school wedding; saving only those essential appointments, orders, and arrangements until the groom returns and doing the rest of them by yourself ahead of time; keeping up on school work and still planning the wedding; etc., etc.

"Two things were invaluable to me in keeping everything according to schedule: 'The Bride's Book of Plans,' and a mimeographed schedule (one for bride, one for groom) of planning a wedding in twelve weeks, which the bridal department of one of the large stores gave me. In the 'The Bride's Book of Plans' I found that the meticulously mapped-out schedule was just the thing for a schedule-minded college senior to follow. In fact, Mother and I were continually referring to it, on the few days that we spent together during the semester!

"I could only add a few things which the two above references did not include. They are: the use of lists for each person concerned with the wedding and reception—attendants, parents, caterers, reception attendants, bride and groom, etc.—lists which give: (1) overnight housing (2) transportation to rehearsal dinner, rehearsal, place of wedding-day meals, church, and reception (3) duties in order. The bride and her mother should keep a master list of all these arrangements at home for reference. Perhaps this is being 'over-organized,' but in that last-minute confusion and deluge of people, it certainly helped us. The other thing I would add, which was not mentioned in my references, is planning for the guests who stay after the reception is over. Our freezer came in very handy here, for Mother had prepared a whole meal for thirty people who might stay—and thirty-two did!

"There are a multitude of details which can be taken care of before the last two weeks, and which should be, especially if

the bride is on her last round of final exams a few days be-
fore the big day. They are: sending stories to the papers which
will do a write-up of the wedding; making out seating charts
for rehearsal dinner; packing clothes for the honeymoon
(with tissue paper so they won't wrinkle) at least a week be-
fore the wedding; making lists of items to take (1) to the
church (2) to the place where you'll change clothes after the
reception and (3) in that one remaining suitcase on your
wedding trip.

"My husband and I found these points useful and helpful to
us

1. We kept our honeymoon plans secret!
2. We did not forget our minister and the religious aspect of
   our marriage in the haste to make it a beautiful affair. He
   was interested in making this a marriage, not just a wedding.
3. An appointment together with the family doctor before
   the wedding.
4. Though we wanted very much to be together those last
   few days before the wedding, we left one night free for
   my family and me. I needed it and they appreciated it.
5. It seemed to us that the more we could discuss items like
   money, in-laws, entertaining, friends, etc., before the wedding, the fewer would be our postmarital problems."

INDEX